The One

A STUDY OF
THE ABSOLUTE

Other Writings by Lillian DeWaters

All Things Are Yours ◆ The Atomic Age
The Christ Within ◆ The Finished kingdom
Gems ◆ God Is All
The Great Answer ◆ Greater Works
"I Am That I Am" ◆ In His Name
The Kingdom Within ◆ Light
Light of the Eternal ◆ Loving Your Problem
The Narrow Way ◆ Our Sufficient Guide
Our Victory ◆ The Price of Glory
Private Lessons ◆ Science of Ascension
The Seamless Robe ◆ The Time Is At Hand
The Understanding Series
The Voice of Revelation
Who Am I ◆ The Word Made Flesh

Available through:
Mystics of the World
Eliot, Maine
www.mysticsoftheworld.com

The One

A STUDY OF
THE ABSOLUTE

Lillian DeWaters

"That they all may be one ... I in them, and Thou in me; that they may be made perfect in one."
—JESUS

THE ONE

First Mystics of the World Edition 2014
Published by Mystics of the World
ISBN-13: 978-0692246450
ISBN-10: 0692246452
Title ID – 4787763

For information contact:
Mystics of the World
Eliot, Maine
www.mysticsoftheworld.com

Cover graphics by Margra Muirhead
Printed by CreateSpace
Available from Mystics of the World and Amazon.com

DeWaters, Lillian, 1883 – 1964
Originally published:
Lillian DeWaters Publications
Stamford, Connecticut, 1927

Contents

"And the glory which thou gavest me
I have given them that they may be one."

Preface

The first textbook in America on spiritual metaphysics, with application to the healing of human problems, was published some fifty years ago, and since the publication of that book, multitudes of writers have used their pens, elucidating many of the "deep things" therein expressed, and have set forth such fuller revelation as appeared to their consciousness.

Nineteen years ago, the one now writing these words published her first book on spiritual metaphysics under the title *Journeying Onward,* and at that time and in that book delivered the basic principles that are to be found in this latest book, *The One.*

During the intervening years the author has written and published over twenty different books, treating the subject—*the Science of Truth*—from various angles and for students and readers of various degrees of understanding.

In her three latest books, called *The Kingdom Series,* the author presented more clearly than in any of her previous writings—*The Finished Kingdom* (reality, or the heavenly world); *The Christ Within* (the nothingness of the personal self); and the understanding that may be demonstrated *In His Name* (the practice of truth).

Now, in this latest work, *The One*, the student will find a delightful union, a gathering, as it were, of all the paramount facts contained in her complete set of writings, making this book a most valuable book for study and for meditation.

In the book *Journeying Onward*, which was published in 1908 and which was one of the first books of its kind to be placed on the market in America, the author set forth in simple fashion the nothingness of personality, the nothingness of belief, the nothingness of sin, sickness, discord, and the oneness of Being, as follows:

"It is our ignorance of God that makes us believe that we lose health and life; the right understanding of God proves that man is forever *at-one* with Him, reflecting all that is in Him and nothing else ... The Master came to save us from believing in sin, sickness, death, and those who are following in his steps are destroying these conditions as he did and are *giving God the glory* ... Sickness seems real to the sufferer, yet it is not a reality, a truth, a right or normal condition of man ... The only devil that one may know is the belief of evil in one's own thought.

"Prayer is realization of possession ... As children of God, *man possesses what God possesses* ... By scientifically understanding these spiritual truths, we are brought into such a consciousness of the allness of God that we behold and receive the manifestation of our desires or prayers ... We try to see so clearly the scientific truth that good fills all space; that all errors or mistakes go out of our thought, and consequently their manifestations disappear ... We strive to be in tune, in touch or harmony with divine Love, so that we may behold *the finished work.*"

What greater vision could one have today than to behold the One—the one Life, the one Power, the one Presence, the one Being? Surely this would demonstrate the love of God, the oneness of man and the kingdom of heaven on earth!

To see the oneness of man transcends malice, jealousy, strife, war, and blesses mankind with the divinity of heaven.

Now, year after year, day after day, we are all approaching nearer and nearer the actual understanding of Truth, and naturally we are all therefore thinking, feeling and speaking more and more alike on this subject. This is in itself a demonstration of the *oneness of man.* What one sees, another sees. What one is having revealed to him, another is also having revealed to him.

Only a short time ago, there arose in our midst a man of daring and skill, a man so detached from any sense of person or personality that he turned his back to any praise and worship directed to his personal self—a praise and a glory directed to him because with his silent winged companion he had triumphed over the dark waters of the Atlantic. As soon as he had demonstrated his vision, others came forward with the same vision and intent.

And today, we read in books, magazines and papers the thoughts and expressions of those who are visioning spiritual heights, visioning the transcension of war, of evil, of death. More clearly, year by year, day by day, this vision will continue, until mankind forgets to struggle; forgets to be selfish; forgets to think of personality, but lovingly all will understand that what blesses one blesses all; that Truth is impersonal; that Truth, when viewed correctly, is loved, worshipped and understood by all alike.

The insight of the hour is the joyous recognition of *the nothingness of personality and the allness of the one Being.* The recognition of *the unity and the oneness of man.*

Laying aside all notion of self and of others, we now bring our willing hearts to worship at the feet of him who gloriously ordained: "That they may be made perfect in one."

—The Author

Labor not with your minds to reach heaven for the way is a laborless pathway. There is but one door—*Believe that ye are already there.*

—*Lillian DeWaters*

CHAPTER I

The Nothingness of Personality

At one time, while this world was considered material, there came into it a voice making the daring statement, "There is no matter; all is mind!"

Slowly Truth comes to this world as though this in itself were a device of redemption.

From the allness of matter to the nothingness of matter and the allness of mind, thence from the allness of mind to the nothingness of mind and the allness of Truth is the path of device to this world.

In the superb view of the heavenly world as here and now and the nothingness of both matter and mind, what might be the next step in illumination? Is there anything else separating man from Truth except the belief in the reality of matter and mind?

After we perceive the nothingness of the world material and the world mental, we can open our eyes to a still larger perception. *We can perceive the nothingness of personality!*

To perceive the nothingness of personality brings speedy deliverance, for it is the angel carrying healing in its wings. It is the angel of Light. It is the angel of the dawn of a new day.

In the glorious vision of the One, is there any room for jealousy, for strife, slander, misunderstanding, unforgiveness? Is there any room for teacher *and* student—for one to be superior to another? Is there anything that I can take from you or you can take from me?

Let us open our hearts wide and wider still to appreciate this stupendous message of the *nothingness of personality,* and let it spread like wildfire from east to west and from pole to pole until the whole earth is compelled through insight and devotion to worship the One.

Let Scientist and Catholic kneel together in this vision of one Being; one Lover of all; loving Jew and Gentile alike. Let the races calling themselves the black, the white, the Indian bow down at this altar and see themselves *as God sees them.*

Think you that God sees the color of a man's skin? Think you that God is concerned whether a church or a sect of people is called Methodist or Baptist? Think you that the One sees *differences?* That the One sees pairs of opposites?

What a glorious day at hand as this great fire of insight begins to blaze and extend over this plane and man begins to see as God sees, and man begins to look upon another as himself, for, in the vision of the One, can there be another?

This is a tremendous light, which, if seen, accepted and *practiced,* will open to one the peace and joy of heaven.

Of what use would it be for one to affirm, "There is but one Being," if at the same time he felt hurt because of what someone said about him unkindly, or if he felt himself unjustly treated by another? Our great need is to *practice* our vision, to *practice* our understanding.

If the One is the All and there is no personality, does not this automatically discharge these deceptions called disease, fear, hate, grief? Can *God* be diseased? Can *God* fear? Can *God* hate? Can *God* be sorry? The One is not emotional but is the stillness of Spirit, unchangeable perfection.

Taking away the sense of personality through insight, through devotion, comes to one as though the veil of the temple had been rent in twain, as though one expected the very ones in their graves to rise and walk about on this plane as though death had never been.

In this transcendent vision of the One, we see only a great family of brethren—each the same Life, the same Substance, the same *Being.* This living fire from heaven bursts into our hearts as though a sheet of lightning were seen and felt, to strike us with its power and glory, touching us with its glow, its ecstasy and its wonder.

When you believe evil about another, where is *your* vision? When you feel injury from another, where is *your* vision?

It is taught by the sages of the East that to be robbed by another is to be a robber in one's own heart; to be killed by another is to be a murderer oneself, which means that if one actually knows and asserts the oneness of all being, he will not see *another* but will see the one Self only, and herein is his protection.

There are statements of Truth to be held in the consciousness as priceless jewels, such as the promises of the 91st Psalm and the promises of the mighty Jesus.

One might, for instance, be placed in seeming danger, his life imperiled, yet if he would declare and know, "Nothing shall by any means harm you," and let this heavenly promise leap from him as living fire from heaven, as veritable Truth Itself, he shall be immune; he shall not be harmed.

Once one had a weapon pointed at him, ready to do him harm, and at that instant he had the vision of the one Being, of this man who held the weapon and of himself as being the *same substance,* the *same Being.* Fearlessly and courageously he asserted this silently to himself, *with no sense of personality,* and the uplifted hand of the man who held the weapon remained in that position, nor could it be moved without the consent of the one who knew the Truth. The knower of the Truth has complete sovereignty.

A man enjoying the charm of an evening's beauty and a high-powered automobile was suddenly confronted by a policeman, who gave him a card with certain accusations against him. The driver, who had harmed no one, felt immediately the presence of the One as the *only* Being. At that very instant the card was snatched from his hand by the policeman, who turned quickly and sped away.

This latter example is not set forth as proof that man should disobey material law but as proof that when man sees as God sees, he is safe. *This is the secret place of the most High.*

Now, if one permits himself to act so as to injure in any way the name or character of another, he is injuring himself, for he is seeing another, whereas, there is no other. With such double vision he finds the injury that he would do another returning upon himself, because oneself is the only self there is.

On the other hand, should one look upon another believing that this other has done an injustice or harm to him, he himself is the guilty one, for were his vision fixed on Reality, he would see no other; he would see no falsity; he would see no injury; he would see only Truth as taking place.

Let us ask ourselves: Is there anything that another can take from me? Is there anyone who can steal from me my joy, my peace, my love, my faith, my understanding? We can but answer truly if we base our decision upon the fact of Life that *God is all there is,* that there is but *one* Presence, *one* Power, *one* Substance, *one* Life, *one* Being.

The cry today as never before is "On the instant." The world wants something that will permit the voice to travel *instantly* from one side of the globe to another; a means that will transport one *directly* from one part of the country to another; a way that will heal another *quickly* of all manner of diseases; a path that will deliver *immediately* from dangers.

What can you announce that would be nearer this end than to know the nothingness of personality and the allness of the one Being?

Can you see that the whole thing, the great farce of evil, rests upon the belief of personality — the belief that man can be separate from God? That man can think other than God? That man can have life apart from God?

If everyone on earth were seeing no distinction, no separateness, no being other than the One, think what instantaneous emancipation this would bring, how the millennium would be in our midst!

No one with a grain of understanding would accuse God of being sick or of being sinful or of dying, yet how many are accusing man of these very things? Therefore, to blot from one's vision one's sense of personality delivers instantaneous illumination, inspiration, healing.

This is actually practicing the Presence, so that if one were looking at an appearance called the devil incarnate and he could know but one Being and the nothingness of any other, he would see before him an angel of Light.

You have heard many times the scientific statement that there is but one man; still, you may not yet clearly understand its deep significance. It means that *inherently* all men are the same. It means that *actually* there is no difference between one man and another. It means that God sees all men alike!

> He maketh the sun to shine on the evil
> and on the good, and sendeth rain on the
> just and on the unjust—Matt. 5:45.

This one Being is the *Father*, Soul, Self, I AM. The *Holy Ghost* is the Light that illumines, inspires, radiates and mirrors forth the *Son*—perfect Man.

As the Father, Self, Soul is infinite, and the Holy Ghost, the Illuminator, the divine Reflector is infinite, so also the Son, the reflection called perfect Man is infinite and is known on earth as sons and daughters, or children of God.

It can be clearly seen that because of the infinity of God the Father and of God the Holy Ghost, we will also have the infinity of God the Son or perfect Man. Thus, man is seen in infinite number, yet understood as one Being.

Jesus, the pivotal character, the miracle-working Presence, stood in the midst of men proclaiming, "And the glory which thou gavest me, I have given *them*, that they may be *one* even as we are *one*."

If one could but place a loving hand upon the shoulder of the man digging a ditch, there would be felt a certain warmth, a loving Presence—Soul answering Soul; or, if one placed this loving touch upon the prisoner in a dungeon, this man's heart would leap, his love would respond, for in every breast abides the *same* Spark, in every life is found the *same* Substance and in every heart there beats the *same* Love. Thus, we recognize the *oneness* of man.

O Spirit, Love Divine, I worship Thee alone,
And besides Thee, I see and claim no other.
I acknowledge Thy Glory as my glory,
Thy Light as my light,
Thy Life as my life,
Thy Self as my self.

As Thyself, Myself, the one and only Self,
I speak forth the word of eternal Reality,
The word of freedom, of unity, of power
    and of glory.

Let him who feels that he is hereby losing his identity hearken closer. Let him who feels that he cannot lose himself listen to the divine decree:

"Except ye be *converted* ye shall not enter into the kingdom. He that *loseth* his life shall find it."

Only he who lays down his life is able to take it up again. And how is one to lose his life, to lose himself? *By seeing the nothingness of personality.* He who lays down his sense of a selfhood apart from God rises up conscious of himself as he *is.*

Personality is man as he *appears,* that is, his habits, his beliefs, his thoughts, his grammar, his clothes, etc. Impersonality is man as he *is.* Truth is impersonal and man is like Truth; man is therefore impersonal.

Suppose one thinks, "I am a great man. I have students to sing my praises over this world, asserting that I am one who imparts truth to others. My name has gone over this planet as a name of importance, as the name of one who knows and understands." What manner of man think you is this?

The man who has lost his life is the man who cares not for himself or his personal name, but his care, his love rests wholly upon the One, like the story related in *The Christ Within* of the man who performed miracles wherever he walked, yet he would not allow his name to be known and was spoken of only as "The Holy Shadow."

When a man "loses his life," what is it that he actually loses? Must he give up his home, his family, his money? Does it mean that he must renounce his joy, his business, his eating, his sleeping?

No, he is not asked to give up any of these things. *Let him give up his sense of a personal self.* Let him lay aside the self that he believes is called "John Doe" and take up that Self that is Truth.

Not only need he have this vision for himself, but such vision must be large enough, full enough to encompass the whole universe, so that he does not see persons as units, as separate beings, but he sees *unity*, he sees the One, only. No matter how many persons are standing before him, he sees the One as the all of each.

> There is neither Jew nor Greek; there is neither bond nor free; there is neither male nor female; for ye are all One in Christ Jesus!

Suppose one is asleep, and in his dream he finds himself stranded on an island. Vainly he looks around for a boat, but there is none in sight. He is without shelter, water or provisions.

Now, the man on the bed and the man representing him in the dream correspond to the true Self and the personality. If the dream character on the island could but know the nothingness of himself, could but give up his life (dream life), such life as he would give up would be nothing in itself, for the personality stranded on the island is not a real existence but is a suppositional one. There would be no actual process taking place, no actual change, nothing really happening, for all the time the self would be on the bed and not on the island.

Thus, when the one known as John Doe gives up his personality, this is not an actual procedure, for what he gives up is *his belief* in a man of matter, a dream substance, a man who is separate from the real Being, when there is no such man! But he goes through this device—this change that is no change, this act that is no act, this awakening that is no awakening—so that he will consciously know the truth about himself.

When the man wakens and finds himself in the bed, then he knows the nothingness of the man on the island. And when man on earth comes into the consciousness of One Being and his identity with this Being, then he knows and understands the nothingness of the man of sin, sickness and ignorance.

With the light of understanding we see then how futile it is to hold to personality, to believe in the personality (dream) man rather than in the true, changeless man of God.

"Except the Lord build the house, they labor in vain who build it" (Ps. 127:1). Except you see, acknowledge, and *practice* that which you actually *are*, your labor to bring success, health, harmony, power, glory to a man of dust, a dream man, a personality man, is all in vain.

It is time all of us who claim to have a grain of true understanding cast aside now and forever all criticism, fear, condemnation of others. We do not criticize and condemn God, and there is nothing else (so we assert). Then whom are we condemning? *The man on the island.*

Now, how foolish it would be for us to look at that man stranded on the island and blame him for his position! The man we would be judging would not be there; he is somewhere else, innocent that very instant, and our ignorant thoughts would but fall back upon ourselves.

Likewise, when we blame others, when we fear others, when we see others, we are but placing fire on our own heads, for the man we are judging or fearing is not present where we are seeing him. He is somewhere else, perfect, innocent that very instant.

He who claims to know truth, let him *live* truth. Let not him who has put his hand to the plow—his vision on the white Christ—look back, for he that is double-sighted is double-minded, and let not that man expect anything from the Lord, his Lordship.

Fear not that in giving up your sense of self you are losing your identity, for lo, you are but finding it; you are but recognizing that which you eternally *are.*

And which would you rather be—John Doe or the Christ-Self? Both we cannot be. Actually, one neither puts off John Doe nor puts on Christ, for what he is not, he cannot lose, and what he is, he cannot put on. Yet this is the way it will seem to him. It will seem as though he were putting on Christ, because he has estimated himself as someone other than the One.

Do you think it makes you love your friend less to know that he is the One rather than that he is John Doe? Not if you love Truth. Instead, we find that our friends, our relatives, our acquaintances, all mean more to us than before. Our love is richer, fuller and is not based upon personality but is based upon the real Substance Itself, so that such love is enduring and eternal.

Is it beginning to be seen and felt by you what a great vision this is, what a stupendous sweep — to behold the nothingness of personality and the allness of the one Being?

I recall the value of this insight to me in a demonstration some years ago. My young child seemed ill with what was called whooping cough. No matter how I kept my thoughts based on Truth it seemed that the child would cough more in my presence than at any other time.

One day while she was sleeping, I entered the room and instantly the coughing began. Meditatively I crossed the room and seated myself by the window. My eyes happened to fall upon a great maple tree directly beneath my vision, and all of a sudden as I beheld the majesty of this tree with its thousands of beautiful green leaves waving in the breeze, a treatment leaped from me, and this treatment was a vision, a revelation of *the oneness of all being and the nothingness of personality.*

Here was the tree filled to overflowing with leaves that were so close together that they were touching one another, yet no leaf depended upon another for a single thing whereby to exist; no leaf had any influence over any other leaf, but each leaf was joined to the branch and the branch joined to the trunk.

This picture was so vivid to me that I instantly saw that no individual on earth depended in any way on another, nor could the life or harmony of any one be influenced by another, for each belongs to the One. With this insight came the instantaneous healing of the child.

Now Truth, revelation, vision, ever descends upon one with healing in its wings. The fire of God is a *consuming* fire, and no one can feel this burning Light, this quickening Spirit, this descent of the Holy Ghost without receiving the blessing.

It is written that the sun shines on the good and on the bad alike, meaning that the sun is not double-minded, double-visioned; so also the light of divine illumination, the Holy Ghost, shines upon the plane called matter as well as the plane of heaven, for Truth sees no distinction, no difference.

When speaking of his Godhood, Jesus announced: "I am the vine; abide in me, for without me, ye can do nothing."

We do not see the leaves fastened to the trunk, but we see the leaves fastened to the *vine,* and the vine to the trunk. Now, as it was the Master himself who gave this illustration, it must present truth, and one must accept the vine, for one cannot come into the fullness of loving understanding except through Jesus Christ and his teaching.

You will notice that they who love Jesus Christ love all mankind. Their hearts have received a glow, a divinity that is not present to him who has not yet felt the Master's touch. There is that bond, that love uniting those who love Jesus Christ, who understand his mission and his presence with us, that nothing else can ever bring.

Those who understand Jesus Christ have their vision away from self, away from personality and upon Reality.

When we worship Jesus Christ, we are not worshipping personality, but we are worshipping the One, for he claimed no goodness of his own, no glory of his own personality, but said, "Whatsoever things the Father doeth, these also doeth the Son likewise ... There is none good but *one*."

Now, when we take a man or a woman of this plane and extol their names and look upon them as specially endowed by God to perform miracles, we are worshipping falsely. We are not worshipping God but are worshipping apart from God. When we want the world to praise us, when we demand obedience from others or feel that we must be loyal to others, where is our vision? On personality.

Let this light of insight blaze over all this world and into the hearts of everyone, that they may see the folly of "authorized" teacher, student or literature. When we are authorized by Truth, we need no other authorization.

Do we read in the Bible that Jesus believed that only those whom he himself instructed should be considered reliable healers and teachers? On the contrary, turning to the gospel of Saint Mark we find that Jesus rebuked his disciples for this very attitude of mind:

And John said, Master, we saw one casting out devils in thy name, and he followed not us, and we forbade him. But Jesus said, Forbid him not ... For he that is not against us is on our part.

Here it is clearly related that the disciples would have practiced what is termed *loyalty* to their teacher, but the matchless Jesus would have none of it.

His vision was ever fixed to Soul that doeth the works, and verifying this unity he further declared, "And the works that I do, ye shall do also," for we are all the same Being.

Where shall *we* place our loyalty? Let each ask and answer this question for himself, but in wisdom let us remember that "No man can serve two masters." We cannot concede a personal teacher or an authorized student and still preserve our clear vision of *one* Being.

Is it not appalling in this day of wonderful revelation that one can believe that another has the right to control him spiritually? We would not consider having another dictate to us as to the food that we must eat for breakfast or the manner of clothing that we must wear on certain days of the week or how we should arrange the furniture in our rooms; then why should we allow another to inform us regarding the spiritual books that we should read in our journey heavenward?

We cannot allow others to govern our spiritual food and at the same time enjoy the presence, the guidance and companionship of the *Spirit within*.

CHAPTER II

The Message of Truth

An illumined one has written the following inspiring words:

"Before the eyes can see, they must be incapable of tears. Before the ear can hear, it must have lost its sensitiveness. Before the voice can speak in the presence of the Masters, it must have lost the power to wound. Before the soul can stand in the presence of the Masters, its feet must be washed in the blood of the heart."

What a world of spiritual food is contained in these words! *Before the eyes can see they must be incapable of tears.* What does this mean? It means that before the inner eye, the eye of Soul beholds for you the oneness of Being, your outer eyes, your senses, must be closed to grief.

Why do we weep tears of grief? *Is it not because of the notion of personality?* Have we not wept because of what people said about us, because of the way they treated us, because of the sense of injustice or hurt that we felt? Have we not wept over our own shortcomings and failures? Have we not wept because of the seeming separation of our loved ones?

Can you see now that all such grief hinges upon the belief of a separate self—a selfhood other than the *One?* If we are seeing and knowing the omnipresence of the one Being, would there be any reason for tears or grief? When we have in us this wondrous vision of the one Being eternally at hand, our eyes will be healed of tears.

Before the ear can hear it must have lost its sensitiveness. Have you not received a message from another that caused you to feel great fear, worry, misery? Have you not heard others speak when their words acted like a knife entering your heart? Have you not listened to gossip, slander, criticism, when it made you confused, fearful, sick? As soon as your inner ear has heard the voice of the Master, the message of Truth, then your outer ears will be dull of hearing.

We must be insensible to the hearing of error, knowing there is but one Voice which speaketh no evil, but is ever Self-conscious, conscious of Its own Being. When gossip, criticism, evil tidings reach our ears and cause not a ripple upon our clear perception of the one and only Being, then we find our joy is complete, is lasting and "no man can take it from us."

Before the voice can speak in the presence of the Masters (the illumined) *it must have lost the power to wound.* Is your voice the voice of a personal being, or is your voice the voice of Truth? When we speak from the consciousness of the one Being and the nothingness of any other being, then our voice carries no power to wound, for it is Truth speaking to Truth.

Before the soul can stand in the presence of the Masters (be conscious of its own glory) *its feet must be washed in the blood of the heart.* Does this mean that we must suffer troubles, agonies, fears, griefs before we can lay claim to a clear perception of the One? Does it mean that experience leads us to Truth? Experience cannot add to that which is already complete, and as we understand this aright we are bathed in the glory of the Lord—we are illumined, we are inspired, we are glorified.

When we see the nothingness of experience, the nothingness of a selfhood apart from God, the nothingness of a world of evil, the nothingness of birth, sin, sickness, death, then our eyes are incapable of tears; our ears have lost their sensitiveness; our voice has lost its power to wound; and our hearts have been bathed in the glory of the Light.

Great men and women of this world may have been led away from the upward vision, the high watch, by not holding fast to the consciousness of the one and only Being, the same in every heart. As soon as the vision sees oneself as greater than another—greater in power, greater in intelligence, greater in authority—that instant one has turned from the light and the glory of Truth.

To see the nothingness of a personal being is to walk in a world of charm and magic, a world of delight and glory, a world peopled with heavenly beings. When we see the self of each one as the one Self then we no longer struggle to outshine, for he who believes himself in any way superior to his fellow men is incapable of discipleship.

All the power there is, all the intelligence there is stands present now for you and for me alike, and no one can lay claim to it more than another.

Now, all the dream of experience asks is for someone to believe in it, someone to bow down and worship it, someone to tremble because of it, someone to run for fear of it. And if one believes in a personal man, he is believing in the dream, and the dream will dance him into trouble until that hour strikes for him when he sees the nothingness of matter, the nothingness of mind, the nothingness of personality and *the nothingness of the dream itself.* Then he is the God-crowned man.

Let us acknowledge Truth in all our ways. Let us acknowledge impersonal man at hand now and here.

The way of redemption is not by way of destruction. "I came not to destroy but to fulfill," spoke he who bathed the feet of his disciples. We are not to eradicate evil from the world. Nor is the world to be healed by right thinking, or people to be made over through methods of concentration and adjustment.

Redemption of the world consists not in healing but in knowing the truth! Redemption consists in knowing the nothingness of the dream rather than in changing the dream.

The way of healing sickness on the material plane is through the device of drugs, knives, climates, etc. This is but changing the dream. The way of healing on the mental plane is through the device of thought, the control of the body through the mind. This, too, aims to bring about a change in the dream; for instance, from the dream of being sick and in trouble to the change called healing.

Changing dreams, while helpful, does not bring the millennium on earth, nor does it take away from the face of the whole world the *notion* of birth, sin, disease, death. Nothing but knowing the allness of Truth and the nothingness of a separate world, the nothingness of a dream world, can bring full emancipation.

We have been taught truly that man actually is a perfect being, living in joy and harmony in heaven and that this earthly existence is like a dream state, fleeting, chimerical. Now, the actual state and the earthly state can be clearly understood through the illustration of our daily experience and our nightly experience, which illustration is as follows:

A man partakes of a hearty meal and lies down in comfort and strength to indulge in quiet sleep. He dreams, and in his dream he finds himself walking along the street very weak and hungry. So feeble is he, so weak from lack of food that he needs to support himself by resting against the side of a building. Now, what shall he do? How can this man in the dream be helped?

One can readily see that the dreamer is laboring under a delusion, for all the time that he believes he is walking on the street, hungry and weak, he is someplace else. He is in his own room, warm, strong, comfortable. He believes he is where he is not, and he is not consciously aware of his right and true position.

Thus man on earth, wandering in a world of birth, change, sin, sickness, death, believes he is where he is not, and he is not consciously aware of his actual, changeless, perfect state in heaven.

It is asked, "How is spiritual treatment given from the Absolute position?" That is, if one does not look to drugs or to right thoughts for healing, then how does one think or act when he practices from the Absolute position?

Continuing the illustration of the man on the couch dreaming that he is walking along the street, faint with hunger, we will assume someone standing by his bedside awake, someone who has the power to know the nature of this man's dream and who sees him weak and faint from lack of food. How shall this man who is awake help the man who is walking on the street faint and hungry?

The answer to this question will also answer the one, "How does the practitioner who knows the truth help the man who comes into his office sick and weak?"

Imagine in his desire to help his hungry friend that the man at the bedside rushes into the kitchen and prepares a hearty meal of delicious food, which he brings on a tray and places by the sleeper, directly at his elbow.

Here then is the sleeper, dreaming that he is famishingly hungry, and here also is his friend, aware of his dream and placing food directly at his elbow. Will this be of any avail? None whatever, for the man who is dreaming that he is hungry has his eyes closed to the plate of food that is touching his elbow.

If only the man who is walking on the street hungry could but know of this plate of sumptuous food! But how can he, since he is but fiction, illusion?

Now, since there is no such man existing as the hungry man on the street, he cannot partake of the plate of food. And the dreamer, the one lying on the couch, why should he partake of food when only an hour previously he dined sumptuously and is not at all weak and hungry, but is strong and perfectly nourished?

Is it clear to you thus far that the man in the dream, hungry, cannot be fed, for there is no such man, and that the man on the bed does not need to eat because he is not hungry?

The idea of bringing the plate of food to the bedside of the sleeper symbolizes *material* means of healing. That is, when one approaches a medical physician for help, this physician fixes his attention on appearances, on the sick body, and he prescribes drugs or operation for the body. He looks *at the picture* and applies his help directly to the picture.

Again, suppose that the man at the bedside of the dreamer has a little more insight into the situation than this and he thinks: "Now, it will do no good to place food at the bedside of this dreamer, for he is not actually hungry, he only *believes* that he is hungry. I cannot help him directly, that is, I cannot help him by forcing the food into his body, for he really does not require food, but I can help him indirectly. As long as it is only belief, if I can change his belief from being hungry to the belief of finding and eating food, he will then have his problem solved."

So, the man awake, standing at the bedside of the man asleep, delivers a *mental* treatment. Paying no heed to the body of the dreamer but fixing his attention upon his *mind*, he speaks to him silently like this:

"Do not stand at the plate glass window of that bakery and starve for food, but go right into the shop, sit down and eat. You will then feel well and strong again."

Without a doubt it is pleasanter, even in a dream, to sit at a table and eat dream food than it is to stand weak and hungry without, but our point of consideration is: how shall one deliver help from the Absolute position?

We have heard that as a man thinketh so he is, inferring that all one has to do is to change his belief and he can be as he will. Now, with such a conception of life, a mental practitioner would not attend to the picture as does the medical physician, for he believes that the way to change the picture is to produce a change in the *mind* of the patient, and then the picture will change automatically.

Using the device of changing thoughts in the mentality has brought better conditions to many, yet it can be readily seen that changing the earthly dream from sickness to health, from poverty to plenty, *has not done away with the dream itself,* for so-called sickness, sin, birth, change, death, continue in this world as previously.

Now, what else is there for the man at the bedside to do? If he does not provide actual food for his friend nor deliver mental treatment to his mind, then how shall he help him, for his desire is to take away this false belief and deliver to him a happy, peaceful experience.

The question is: If I do not use drugs, material means directly upon the body of one who claims sickness, and if I do not direct my right thoughts to his mind, endeavoring to change his thought from sickness to health, then what is the way? How shall I proceed if I ignore both the body and the mind of the patient?

The words of the master physician are still vibrant in this world today, "Know the truth and the truth shall make you free!"

One immediately asks, "But how can I know without thinking?"

"Take ye no thought, for in an hour when ye think not, the Son of man cometh (the Truth is revealed to you)."

How can one know without thinking?

This question may be answered by asking another. How can one get into a mirror without getting into a mirror?

When you wish to see how you look, you stand before a mirror, do you not? There is no labor attached to this. You do not put a hole in the mirror to make room for your reflection. You do not have to throw yourself at the mirror or put forth any effort whatsoever. You merely *stand still before the mirror* and it is done. Without acting, without thinking, there you are in the mirror!

How can one know anything and still not think? Now, the mind is like a mirror; it *reflects*, and when one knows Truth, it has nothing whatever to do with his mind any more than there is a connection between a person and the mirror, but the mind reflects Intelligence and as one gets into the mirror so to speak, without effort or strain, so does one know the Truth without an actual process of thought taking place at all. This is what is called spiritual Consciousness.

Take ye no thought! You do not go to the mirror to see how or why that image of yourself is there, for you cannot find out. The picture in the mirror is not coming out of the mirror. The image in the mirror is seen there because you are standing *before* it, and likewise true thoughts come not from the mentality, but are seen and felt in the mentality because one is standing before the Light!

This is the great principle of reflection, which enables us to see ourselves as we *are*, see ourselves in the finished kingdom.

"Look unto Me" is the command of the super world, the message of Truth. Turning away from all else, one looks steadfastly into heaven, reality, and immediately his mind is flooded with thoughts of love, wholeness, abundance, joy, peace and glory.

God is the Holy Ghost, the great Light, and as man looks into this Light, what does he see? What can anyone see who looks into the white mirror but *himself*? And so man sees Himself, and his mind is lighted and his body is lighted, and still he has been "thoughtless."

To see clearly that thoughts of Truth do not spring from the mentality; that knowing Truth is not a conscious mental process but is the *act of Truth Itself*; to look to Soul, to the only Being there is, rather than to attend to one's mind, is to come into a clear vision, a new country.

To see that thoughts of Truth come from Truth, Soul, and not from mentality is to experience great joy and freedom.

We should surely have and enjoy true thoughts with no more labor than we breathe the air or expand our lungs. The act of Truth is not a motion, not a process, not a method, not a procedure. It has nothing whatever to do with time and space, but it is Self-consciousness, Truth knowing Itself— spiritual Consciousness!

Therefore, to "know the truth" does not mean to deliberately, consciously use the mind to formulate thoughts as one would grind out coffee from a coffee mill, but knowing the Truth is that paradox wherein it is stated, "When I am weak, then am I strong!"

Here now we have the man standing by the bedside of his sleeping friend, wishing to help him, wishing to use the highest practice and hearing the words of the all-knowing Jesus, "Ye shall know the truth, and the truth shall make you free."

What is the truth that this man is to know for his friend? He is to know, first of all, that his friend dined but a short time ago, that he is not hungry and that he does not need any food. This is the simple truth. He does not know this in order that the man will stop being hungry, but on the contrary, he knows this because he recognizes that this is the truth.

As he sees the man in the dream wandering on the street, weak and hungry, he knows that it is only a picture man having no substance to it whatsoever, for there is his friend right before his eyes, lying quietly and peacefully on the bed. Therefore, he is not deceived by appearances.

He does not go out into the dream and take the dream man into a dream restaurant; neither does he direct mental treatment to his mind, thereby to assuage his hunger; but he stands still, facing the truth, knowing that both the dream and the man in the dream are nothing and knowing the safety and wholeness of the man where he *actually is.* The dream, which is nothing, being only a picture in the mind of the sleeper, then ceases.

With this illustration in mind we come now to the practitioner of Truth who has before him a patient asking for help. It may be that this one says he is sick or sorrowful or fearful. Such is the picture man who approaches the one who is to help him.

The practitioner, using the highest practice, has taken for his foundation, "The Truth is all there is, and besides the Truth there is nothing else." Therefore, who is this that approaches him? Is it a being called John Doe who is sick and in trouble? How can this be, if Truth is all?

The practitioner is not deluded into administering treatment to the sick body or the sick mind, but with vision fixed clearly on the truth of Being, the Rock of Ages, *he knows the nothingness of mortal mind and mortal man, and he understands the oneness and omnipresence of perfect Being.* He knows that when he looks upon what seems a sick man, there is no such man present, any more than there was a hungry man in the dream.

Therefore the highest practice, the mount of fulfillment, is simply *knowing the truth,* knowing the allness of perfect Being and Its reflection and knowing the nothingness of any other being or belief. Such knowing is not an operation of mind or a process of thought, but is *spiritual consciousness —* Self, conscious of the allness and oneness of Being.

Why is it that the one called patient will find himself restored to harmony? Because of the nothingness of his dream and the oneness of man. When one man knows the truth, it includes the one called patient, for man is one. This oneness is the love of God.

Man knows the truth not with cold reason and logic, but with love and faith. It is as one looks with the vision of a pure heart, as one recognizes the Jesus Christ presence as the One and Only, that he is able to see the nothingness of dreams, of shadows, of fiction.

The practitioner clearly perceives the nothingness of personality; the nothingness of any self separate from God; the nothingness of any mind but the

divine Mind or Intelligence, which does not dream;
the nothingness of any body but the body of Truth,
the image and likeness of God.

It is our ignorance of God, Truth, that brings
forth these dream pictures of good and evil, right
and wrong, but the understanding of the one
Being enables us to lay hold upon reality, which is
at hand, untouched by any dream about It.

Now, spiritual man is not in this apparent
world any more than you are in your dream.
When you dream that you are across the ocean,
you never actually leave your couch, nor does
spiritual man exist in a false world—a world of
birth, change and death. Spiritual man is never
born, is never sick and never dies.

When in your sleep you believe that you are
falling off a precipice or running from a wild
animal, the precipice and the wild animal exist
only in your mind, in your belief, and so are
wholly mental. Your fear, your suffering in the
dream is entirely a mental state, self-created,
although you are ignorant of this fact.

You do not actually leave your couch to fall
off a precipice; you leave the couch *in belief only*,
which is the same as not leaving it at all!

You see this clearly and accept it without
protest. So in this world, when man reports pain,
sickness, trouble, you must also clearly perceive

that it is in his mind only, self-created, although he is ignorant of this fact, while all the time he is a perfect being living in a perfect world!

Man does not actually leave heaven, the perfect state of life, in order to experience pain in a false world, and to live in a false world *in belief* is the same as not living in a false world at all!

This insight shows one clearly the nothingness of *mind,* the nothingness of *belief,* the nothingness of *experience* and the nothingness of *false man.*

Chapter III

Mortal Mind and Matter Explained

Now, truth does not proclaim that the way out of falsity is to waken from actual sleep or dream; that is, the way of deliverance is not by actual awakening, for to admit an awakening would be to admit actuality of the dream.

Students often say, "I know that I am only in a dream of sickness, but I must get out of the dream."

They are asked by the teacher, "What is the treatment for man in a dream or in an illusion?" And they answer, "Waken him."

Let it be clearly seen and understood that such a notion is not Science, for there is no actual awakening to take place, and should one attempt to waken another from a dream or sleep, he betrays that he himself is deluded.

The right treatment for what seems to be man in a dream or delusion is this: "There is no man asleep in a dream!"

You see, the belief that man is in a material world or is in a dream or in a sickness is a falsity, a lie, a deception, and must be denounced. Man is not to be taken out of the dream, out of the sickness, out of the false world, but man is to know that he cannot be deluded, and he is to know that a false belief is nothing at all, *nothing at all!*

Is it evident to you now why Jesus said, "Take ye no thought," and "Ye shall know the truth and the truth shall make you free"? Thought of any kind cannot deliver a dream man, for such a man is nothing, no substance. Nor can any kind of thought place a man where he already is.

To know the truth means to see through a deception! To know the truth means to have the spiritual insight which frees you from a false belief!

Attempting to waken oneself or another from evil brings about no deliverance, and trying to take away sickness from what seems a sick man is the very same as endeavoring to feed the hungry man in the night dream.

Suppose that one meets a man who is sick and is crying out for help. Should he look upon this sick man, affirming, "Now, this man is not really sick or in pain; he is only sick in a dream existence," the man would continue to cry for help. But suppose another, seeing the sick man and hearing his cry for help, knows, "There is no dream world. There is no man in a dream world. There is no man suffering in a dream world." The suffering would cease, for this man would be "knowing the truth." The emancipator is truth.

It may be asked, "Why do we hear so much about the night and the day dream? Why talk in parables and illustrations? Why not give plain answers to plain questions?

You will notice that the infallible Jesus talked in parables. He did this for a reason, and the reason is this: The mind will not function to a parable.

When one relates a story or a parable, it is the same as though the listener were looking at a picture. He perceives. He recognizes. His mind is without thought, is quiet, still, while he is *perceiving* the facts that are being laid out before his vision. Insight, discernment is taking place, and when the story is finished he says simply, "I see. I understand. It is clear to me."

Such understanding has not come to him over the track of his intellect, but through Soul-perception. All teachers who present the science of the Absolute, the science of perfection at hand, follow the great Master and teach by means of illustrations and parables, for only when the mind is thoughtless does insight take place.

Now, how does all this apply to healing the sick? Well, if one is able to perceive the *nature* of sickness, he will be in a fair way to become or continue a well man, whereas, if one is shown through mental reasoning how to destroy sickness, although he may recover from that particular ailment, he is liable to have troubles under other names at other times, for emancipation consists not in destroying dreams, not in destroying false or evil conditions but in *understanding their nothingness.*

Thus we see why it is that man cannot actually be healed; why it is that we are not to attempt by any means whatsoever—material, mental or spiritual—to destroy evil. We see that man cannot actually be taken from this world and its trouble, *because he is not actually in it.*

This is the reason that so-called disease continues throughout the world regardless of all the material remedies of drugs and operations and with all the mental remedies of right thoughts at hand.

As long as there are physicians and healing means, there will be conditions to be healed. All sickness is but false belief in the human or carnal mind, and those who would heal sickness are those who believe it is something to be healed. Thus it can be seen that the only way to be rid of what is termed disease is to *disbelieve* in it.

The only way that you can get a picture into a mirror is to place an object before the mirror.

The only way to see the picture called disease in the world is to believe in disease, for the picture of disease is the externalization of the belief. Belief is that which casts the picture and without belief there could be no corresponding reflection or picturization.

If all the world would have spiritual insight to discern that all picturization of evil and trouble in this world is but the shadow of ignorance, false belief, and would refuse all healing means and simply "know the truth,"—which is, know the nothingness of belief, the nothingness of deception, the nothingness of dream and dreamer—and would acknowledge the allness and omnipresence of perfect man in a perfect, changeless world, all false pictures, like dreams, would vanish away, and man would find himself in heaven, living his actual life.

All kinds of devices have been used in this world to free man from sickness and trouble. Belief or faith, however, in the means employed is absolutely necessary in effecting a cure or a help, no matter what the aids are that are applied.

We hear the voice of the Master, "All things are possible to him that believeth!"

When man is dreaming that he is in the ocean, will his belief that he is in his own room bring him back to his bed? No. But if he could believe this in his dream, it would be a device that would cause the dream to cease. Thus belief as a device is used in aiding man to experience freedom.

When the sick use drugs, for instance, and they later say that they have been helped or healed, how has this come about? Is there any power in medicine? No. God *alone* is power. The drug does not heal because of any intrinsic value it contains, but the person taking the drug has belief either in the physician who recommends it or in the drug itself, or perhaps belief in both, and this belief is a device, detaching him from his sense of sickness and often effecting a cure.

Since man is already in heaven now and man is never sick except in belief (which is not at all), he must also be healed only in belief. He cannot *actually* be healed, for he is not *actually* sick. He cannot actually be placed in heaven, harmony, for the kingdom of heaven is *already* within him.

Thus man is healed only in belief, whether he places his faith in drugs, in right thought or in Truth. One might ask, "Then why not accept medicine instead of studying Truth?" For this reason: One uses medicine to destroy or heal sickness, and even though he is cured of a particular ailment this way, still he is liable to other ailments at any moment.

One studies Truth that he may experience uninterrupted harmony; that he may enjoy absolute freedom; that he may clearly perceive the *nothingness* of all dreams of sin, sickness and death and demonstrate continual peace, joy and harmony.

Many students have the idea that they must continually be seeking Truth. They read, study, take instruction with the idea that they are seeking for something — seeking for Truth, that is, that Truth is something for which they are looking, something which they would add to their being, some appendage, like a cloak that they would wrap around them. Now, this is not the right understanding of it.

I recall at one time, when I was earnestly trying to make a demonstration and it did not come to pass, that I felt all the time that it *must* come to pass, that I *must* prove the truth. Then one day like a flash it came to me this way: "It is not you proving truth, but it is Truth proving *you!*" What a difference it makes, and how it turns us directly around.

We look out when we should look *in*. How wonderful, how restful, how glorious it is to meditate upon the fact that Truth knows Itself. Truth is forever conscious of Truth and of nothing else.

We need not seek Truth as though we were looking for something that is hidden afar off, as something which we would add to ourselves, for when we come into the light of true understanding we find that Truth is right at hand, nearer than our breathing, for we ourselves are Truth. Truth is our life, our substance, our very being.

Now, we have heard that mortal mind is all that believes in sickness or evil and that mortal mind alone creates it. Many may not have a clear understanding of what constitutes mortal mind.

The greatest of all teachers said, "How can one enter a strong man's house and spoil his goods except he first bind the strong man?" This "strong man" is of course the mind.

Some people use the term *mortal mind* as though it were a personal being or a personal devil, as though it were some thing or mind or being that acted against them, causing them to do what they should not do and to be what they should not be. Now, mortal mind, or the human mentality, can be clearly explained and understood.

We know that God, divine Mind, Truth, does not create or sustain evil. If we assert that evil is the product of mortal mind and then claim the nothingness and fabulous existence of both mortal mind and evil, how are such ideas to be accepted and understood?

Let us imagine that the people of the whole universe, or a vast portion of it, are asleep, dreaming. In their dreams are millions of people wandering around in pleasure, pain, good and evil experiences. In their dreams are houses, streets, land, water, sun, stars, cities, animals, people. Did God create these? No. Are they real? No. Have they any substance? No. Have they any life? No. Who created them? The dreamers. Is the universe which one dreamer creates any different from the universe that another dreamer creates? No. They are both the same—both *nothing.*

Is this not so? That is, it matters not who the man is that is doing the dreaming, whether a lord or a peasant, the dreams are springing from the same source.

Is Soul the dreamer? Does Truth, the real Self, dream? No. Then what is it that dreams—that produces cities where there are no cities, that creates men and women where there are no men and women, that creates a whole universe where there is no such universe? The mind of the sleeper.

Since the dream of one dreamer is the same as the dream of another dreamer, we can group all dreams together and state that "mind is the dreamer." The mind brings forth a false, an untrue, an unreal creation which has no life, no substance, no being whatsoever, but is wholly hallucination, deception.

We can easily admit that man, in a dream, can feel pain when there is no pain, can be afraid when he is in no danger and has no reason to be afraid. For instance, one might dream that he broke his arm and that a surgeon came and set the bone and a nurse took charge of the case.

Now, all the time that he is feeling his arm broken, set and bandaged, his arm is actually thrown carelessly over his head on his pillow, safe and sound, yet he is in total ignorance of this fact. To him his arm is broken when it is not broken; he is feeling pain when there is no reason for pain whatsoever; he is living in a false world, in a false belief, cut off from this world and from this self.

Now, since divine Mind, Intelligence, does not sleep or dream, then we state that one's mind sleeps and dreams and one cannot actually be shut off from this world while in dreams, but that one can be shut off only in *belief*. In belief man has a mind that weaves falsities, deceptions, which have nothing whatever to do with his actual existence in his room and bed. At night, then, he is exiled from this world and this self through what is called a dream in the mind.

We come now to man in this world awake, exiled in belief from heaven. Blinded to the facts of Life, he finds himself in a world of change, sickness, trouble, evil, with a body that feels sensation, pain; with a mind that thinks thoughts of fear and worry; with changes, earthquakes, accidents taking place over which he seems to have no dominion. Now, who is responsible for all this, and how is one to be delivered?

There are questions which have been asked ever since the dream of belief began and some day must be answered so that the entire world will understand. Man is an intelligent being and is to know the truth about himself and the universe.

We can plainly see that there is no actual way by which man can be delivered in his night dream from the broken arm, for the simple reason that the arm is not broken. Even waking him will not actually deliver him, for there is nothing actual from which he is to be delivered. *But waking him from the dream will cause him to see the unreality of the dream experience and the reality of the truth at hand.*

Let man use his intelligence to see that as the night dream of sickness is unreal and for this reason can be destroyed, so also the day dream of sickness is unreal and for this reason can be destroyed. We have a heaven, at hand, present, not any distance away, in which man lives. He is exiled from this heavenly world, not actually, but in belief, only, and to waken to the *nothingness of belief* delivers one to the reality which is here and now.

When man breaks an arm in his waking hours, he calls a surgeon, has the bone set, feels the pain, etc. Where is this experience taking place? In heaven? No. It is taking place in what has been called *mortal existence.*

The mortal body has been hurt, for surely the spiritual body could not be hurt. Whose mortal body? The mortal (dream) body of the mortal (dream) mind. What is this mortal or carnal mind and to whom does it belong? It is nothing in and of itself, and it belongs to no one. It is *fabulous* and can well be compared to the mind of the man in the night dream.

The man in his dream at night, finding himself in the office of the surgeon, having a bone set— what man is this? This is a false man. There is no such man at all.

And the mind that is feeling the pain in the arm—whose mind is this? It is a false mind. There is no such mind at all. It does not belong to the man on the bed, for you might speak to him and ask him where he is and if he is in pain, and hearing you, he would answer that he is not feeling any pain at all, that he is in his own room and in no danger whatsoever.

To be able to see the nothingness of this *man* with a broken arm in the dream, and to also see the nothingness of the *mind* thinking, believing this experience, is the insight which leads you to see the similar relationship between man on earth and man in heaven.

The dream man in the physician's office typifies *mortal man,* a belief man, a picture man, a man with no substance, no life, no actual being whatsoever.

The mind that is sustaining this dream man in the physician's office typifies the mind of the sick man on earth, and this mind has been called carnal mind or *mortal mind.*

After one clearly perceives and accepts this illustration, then the next step for him to take is to acknowledge the *nothingness* of the dream man with the broken arm in the physician's office, and the *actuality* of the man with his arm thrown carelessly over his head on the pillow, which symbolizes the *nothingness* of a mortal man walking on this earth sick, poor, troubled, and the *actuality* of man living, moving, acting in the spiritual world, happy, whole, harmonious.

To have the spiritual insight to understand this explanation is like putting wings to one's feet, sweeping him into a new country, delivering lightness to his being, power to his acting and joy to his heart.

Matter is the name given to the body that is born, that is sick, that dies, apparently. *Mortal mind* is the term applied to the mind that manifests such a body, the mind that *believes* in disease, sin and death. Matter is the externalization of mortal mind, and they are one, which one is nothing actual, nothing eternal, nothing real, consequently is dreamlike only.

The mind that is thinking, "I am sick, I am sinful, I am weak," is a false mind, a mortal mind, a dream mind, for of course, it is not the mind of God, which is the *only* Mind, and this dream mind externalizes or shadows forth what is called disease and pain in the body.

Now, to see and to accept that such mortal mind is nothing, nonexistent, and that its mortal conditions are nothing, nonexistent, is to be free from the false claim.

It should be easy now for one to clearly understand these illuminating words from the pen of the noted writer and teacher of spiritual Science:

> "Asserting a selfhood apart from God is
> a denial of man's spiritual sonship ... This
> carnal, material mentality, misnamed mind,

is mortal ... You command the situation if you understand that mortal existence is a state of self-deception and not the truth of being ... False sense evolves, in belief, a subjective state of mortal mind which this same so-called mind names *matter*, thereby shutting out the true sense of Spirit ... Matter is but an image in mortal mind ... The human mind and body are myths ... This phantasm of mortal mind disappears as we better apprehend our spiritual existence and ascend the ladder of life."

O wonderful Light! O glorious insight transcending us, opening our vision to the nothingness of evil, the nothingness of false minds and false bodies, the nothingness of pictures and dreams, and beholding for us the omnipresence of the one eternal Being, the one eternal Perfection here and now!

CHAPTER IV

Removing the Veil

Imagine a number of people meeting together and planning an idea to fool and frighten others. Suppose that in an empty room they scheme to fashion a great and terrible looking figure. The room is empty, typifying nothingness. Nothing is there. Nothing is present.

Presently one man brings in a piece of cloth and some sticks, and in this nothing (emptiness) he commences to fashion a shape, an appearance. Others bring horns, shoes, canes, veils, etc. At last a great giant dragon is formed, terrible to look upon, reaching to the ceiling and appearing ready to spring ferociously upon one.

Now, the first one to enter this room, entirely ignorant of what is there, seeing this frightful being, is so terrified for the moment that his heart stops beating and he is carried out lifeless.

Others coming in contact with this dragon-appearance meet their fates, and many who escape have diseases come upon them and fearful thoughts which never leave them. Soon report spreads over the whole earth that anyone coming into the presence of this being will meet with great sorrow, trouble, evil of all kinds.

Now, all this time this being is but a *false* being, a *false* appearance; yet, because of man's belief in it as something real, something actual, evil results are manifested. Not because of the being itself but *because of the fear and belief in it,* disasters ensue.

Now, for ages and ages this farce continued, yet all the while it was prophesied that someone would come — a Redeemer, a Christ, a Savior who would bring salvation, deliverance. At last the time arrived. He came. He spoke boldly and fearlessly to the people. He told them that sickness was the result of their own belief in this devil which he denounced as a liar, a deceiver from the beginning.

He frightened disease and evil beliefs so that they ran screaming with terror. He healed great multitudes of all forms of diseases and taught them marvelous things about life.

Finally, one day this Savior came face to face himself with this devil that everyone feared. Entering the presence of this great make-believe, he challenged it thus: You have no real power at all. I can look back and see your beginning from nothingness. For this cause came I into this world, that I should bear witness unto the Truth, that I might destroy the works of the devil, that I might be the Savior of the world. I came not to judge the world but to save the world. Kill me, destroy this temple called body, and in three clays I will raise it up from the grave, for I came to give my life a ransom for all, that they should no longer remain in ignorance and darkness but should live in the light of Truth!

Now, when this false being was thus challenged there began a terrible warfare. Because of men's belief in this devil and the great hate that this aroused, this Christ, this Savior was taken away and put to death.

The sun now stopped shining and the whole earth was plunged into a terrible darkness. It seemed as though the universe itself would be rent asunder as an earthquake convulsed the earth, tearing great rocks in pieces and even opening graves of many.

It was then that all the sorcery, all the mystery, falsity, belief and fear connected with this devil crashed into oblivion through the insight and understanding of this mighty redeemer, who gave himself a ransom for the whole world.

All hail! Behold the king! He came forth from the grave announcing, "I have the keys of death and hell!" And, Jesus, the Redeemer, was crowned with glory so that one could scarcely look upon his face for the wonder of it, and through death he destroyed him that had this seeming power over the people. No wonder the proclamation, "All nations shall call him blessed."

And this victorious Christ said to all people, for all time to come, that since he proved the nothingness of this devil that they should no longer have any fear or any belief in it.

Now, dear ones, who read these lines and are running away from the devil that has been modernized into words *mortal mind, animal magnetism, error*—come and see its nothingness. How can there be God Almighty and something besides?

When we fight sickness, sorrow and trouble, it is the same as though we were fighting a frame-up being in the room. It does no good. Yet could we but stand in the presence of such an appearance and have a suspicion, an inkling that it might not be actual after all, and could we but pull off a veil, a stick, and keep on and on until it was all uncovered, what would be left? Nothing—error reduced to nothingness.

What greater blessing can we bring to the world than help expose the falsity of any power apart from God?

Insight delivers! Insight frees—not from evil but from *belief* in evil!

Therefore the truth proclaims: A false man is nothing! A false mind is nothing! A false manifestation is nothing! The true man, the real manifestation, the world of joy and peace and love and glory is the finished work which is changeless, eternal, here and now!

Always, in an unreal experience, one is seeing and feeling his own mental creation. For instance, if one were dreaming that he stood upon the shore of a lake, if he would, he could say to himself, "Now, I can dip my hands into this water; I can feel how cold it is, I can taste it—and still the fact is that I am not seeing water; I am not feeling water; I am not tasting water, for there is no water present except what I myself am creating in mind."

Again, this dreamer might find himself standing beneath a fruit tree which was in full bloom, and he would be distinctly aware of the fragrance of its blossoms; and if he would, he could say to himself, "Now, here is this fruit tree loaded with blossoms, whose fragrance scents the air, yet this tree occupies no space at all. There are no blossoms here, no trees here, and the idea that I am standing here is also only fiction, for I really am not here at all."

Now, one can look at this world of change and say and feel the same. When one notices the leaves fading and falling, when one sees change, accident, discord, death, really this is only fiction, for Spirit informs us that all is changeless good, that the kingdom of perfection is right in our midst, and there is only one presence, power, activity, being.

Such is the wisdom one knows when he stops his mental thinking founded upon his senses and perceives instead the facts of Life.

As it is possible for one in losing his life to find it, and for one while walking in the midst of the sea to find himself on dry land, so is it possible for one believing himself to be living in a world of beginning and end to find himself actually in heaven.

If one would investigate or study or attempt to understand this material world, this thinking mind, this aging body, he must turn his attention in an opposite direction; the same as if one were to study a rose, to understand the history and construction of a rose, he would not sit before a mirror and study the rose in the mirror, but he would turn his attention in an opposite direction—he would look to the rose standing *before* it.

Likewise, instead of looking to the mind or the body, one must look in the opposite direction— one must study the world *within*.

For illustration: One might in his dream find himself in a great palace. He is being conducted through this place of splendor and grandeur by the architect, by the one who says that he drew the plans, that he conceived the ideas which culminated in this massive structure.

Minutely the man in the dream examines the walls, the painting, the marble stairs, the furniture and rugs, and his praise and amazement know no bounds as he walks from room to room, from floor to floor, marveling at the greatness, the skill, the art and beauty of the building.

Turning to the architect, he asks, "And how long did it take to build this greatness, to lay these boulders, to erect these steeples?"

"Five years," was the reply. And the man in the dream assents, "Yes, it must have taken that time."

Ah, but he is looking in the wrong direction! He is studying the roses in the mirror. He is looking at an outside world, and if he but turned his attention in an opposite direction, if he but looked *within*, what a different world he would find, how differently he would view creation.

In studying the outside world, he is greatly deceived. He believes what is not true at all. He believes that five years have elapsed from the beginning to the completion of this palace, that hundreds of men were employed, laboring with their heads and hands to furnish such splendor, whereas, if he but turned his vision *within,* he would snap his fingers and exclaim:

"Aha! This place was made on the instant. I see that with no time at all, these great boulders were placed in position, these high walls were erected, these gold steeples were raised, these massive doors were hung, these rugs were made and placed upon the floors."

Then, looking upon the man who claimed to be the architect and slapping him upon the shoulder, he would cry, "Ha! It was not you who designed this, not you who created it, but it was I! I did it all. I drew the plans with my *eyes closed.* I placed the boulders and erected the steeples with my *hands folded.* I secured the lumber, the brick, the marble, the furniture *without moving.* I, I, alone created, conceived, erected, furnished this stupendous structure *on the instant, without labor, without action, without thought!"*

O how wonderful, how thrilling, how different when man looks within, when he sees the naked truth, when he understands the nothing-ness of an external world!

Can you not recall dreaming about some great danger from which you wished to flee, and for some unknown reason you found that you could not move your feet, that they were "rooted to the spot?" Have you not also in your dreams felt that you would like to scream and shout, yet you could not open your mouth, you could not utter a single sound? Just see how ridiculous this is, that you can be bound without being bound, that you can be tied without being tied.

Can you see clearly that such mental bondage is no bondage—is nothing? For all the time that one feels in his sleep that he cannot move, he could easily spring instantly from his bed? *Mental slavery, mental ignorance is pure deception.*

It is exactly the same in the waking state as in the sleeping state. Those who sit in their chairs feeling that sickness binds them there are being fooled. They are suffering from mental ignorance, for all the time they have a perfect body, luminous as the sun, light as the air.

In the waking state matter appears to be resistant, that is, if we wish to walk out of a closed room we do not pass through the wall or door but we open the door. We feel that a closed door obstructs our passage. But did Jesus feel this way? Did he not pass through walls and doors, and did he not promise that the works that he did, *we* could do also?

No change took place in the walls through which Jesus passed. They did not crumble and fall, nor did he leave a hole in them as he passed through them. They were exactly the same after he passed through them as before. What is it that makes it possible for one to accomplish what seems impossible to another, even though we are all the same being? *Viewpoint.* One man is seeing that the so-called material world is not actually material or external to him, but that it is a mental world, *a world within his own mind,* exactly as is the world in the mind of the dreamer.

As the roses in the mirror are not actually in the mirror, so the world that is called external and resistant is not actually external and resistant.

As one in the night dreams, realizing that he is dreaming can have the dream *as he pleases* — can fly through the air, can become visible and invisible, can speak and have it come to pass — so also one in the waking state, or human experience, understanding that man is not actually in an external material universe but that the universe is within man, can have his world as he pleases, can speak and have it come to pass.

Therefore, it is the way one looks at a thing, at a condition, at a world, that counts.

The man who sits before the mirror studying the form, color, substance of the roses in the mirror is deceived from the start. His vision is *out* instead of *in;* his viewpoint is incorrect.

The man who stands before the world of reflection knowing the facts, having the veil removed from before his eyes, is master of that reflected world.

Now, man on the material plane may commit sin according to that plane of estimation, but when he has a vision that transcends that plane, he does not thereafter continue in that sin, but on the contrary, that practice at once ceases or drops away from him.

Under the perception of Truth, evil does not continue in our lives but is promptly reduced to nothingness, and the practice of evil is discontinued. They who believe that their understanding of the nothingness of evil permits them the license to further indulge in evil with no ill results, sooner or later discover their mistake.

Practicing evil in the name of good is not according to spiritual insight or spiritual understanding. The mind is the source of all experience. It has therefore been proclaimed that the wrong thinking of this mind results in the evil that is seen in this world, that is, all evil, sin, disease, death are caused by wrong thoughts, and to correct or rectify or destroy such conditions, one must introduce the antidote—right thinking.

Under such condition right thought would then produce heaven. Right thought would be the deliverer. Right thought would be the Redeemer, the Christ. But such teaching is not truth!

As drugs and surgical operations open up paths of escape in the human experience, they serve a purpose and are oftimes helpful. Then, as one emerges from the material plane of material means and methods of deliverance, he may adopt the mental remedy of mental law, applying right thought to his mental experience. And without a doubt, right thought is a great step in advance of material means and is a helpful device leading into happier ways and experiences.

Multitudes in this world have laid aside drugs and medicines, as children lay aside their blocks and dolls. And multitudes in this world today are opening their vision preparatory to the laying aside of mental means and methods for something still higher—*for spiritual understanding.*

As mental means, known as right thinking, transcend material means and methods, likewise does spiritual understanding transcend mental means and mental methods. Spiritual consciousness brings forward, introduces, no device, no means, no method. *It stands alone! It is Self-supported!* Spiritual consciousness is Self-conscious of Its aloneness, of Its allness. It is the light of Light! It is the power of Power! It is the act of Truth! It is the removal of the veil.

The kingdom of heaven is not the product of anyone's right thinking, nor is right thought the vehicle delivering one to heaven.

Let man open his vision to perceive that he is *already* in heaven, even though apparently dwelling on earth; that all kinds of means for healing, whether material, mental or spiritual, will continue to be used, only finally to be cast aside, for man will tear off veil after veil, covering after covering until he sees *face to face*—until he recognizes the One as the All-in-all.

Then he may seem to rise from the dead, to awaken as it were from a dream and find himself in the only world in which he ever lived, the perfect world, the city of God, the finished kingdom.

As man thinketh, so is he in belief, and as man understandeth so is he in truth. You can easily see that at nighttime in the dream one enters a world that is nonexistent. He sees, feels, hears things which are not external and which exist only in his own mind. And it must be the same in this dream of material existence—that we are living in a world that is nonexistent, a world that is not external to us but exists only in our own mind. We see, hear, feel things which have no actuality in Truth, hence no actuality at all. It must be that as one can be shut off from this world in the night dream, although he does not go out of it, so one is shut off from the spiritual world, heaven, although he never leaves it.

It has been said that man looks out upon the spiritual world the same as he looks out from his bedroom window upon the world before him. Looking from this window he can see the world only inasmuch as this window will allow. He can see only what is within a radius of his vision. There are miles of land, there are trees and skies which are near enough to him but which he cannot see, owing to the diminutive size and position of the window.

Now, after this fashion man looks out into the land of Truth. He can behold only according to his spiritual vision, according to the opening through which he is looking. Could he but tear the veil from his vision, rend the covering from his eyes, he would see face to face; he would see as God sees; he would behold perfect man and perfect universe.

CHAPTER V

Absolute Science

Absolute Science is the message of the finished kingdom at hand, now. It is not the science of health, but it is the science of wholeness. It is not the science of right thinking, but it is the science of Intelligence. It is not the science of mind over matter or mind over mind, nor is it the science of progression or evolution.

Absolute Science delivers the message of perfect God and perfect Man, *one Being,* untouched by any dream or belief. It is the science of illumination, the science of insight and under-standing.

"I came to redeem and not to destroy," uttered the Lord of heaven and earth. The way to redeem unreality is to see that it is unreality. The way to redeem a dream is to see that it is a dream. *"Only believe,"* entreated he. The door out of a dream is the door of true belief, for true belief leads to understanding.

Redemption is vision, perception, understanding that one cannot destroy the things in a dream, that one cannot destroy a shadow or an illusion. Renunciation is giving up ignorance, giving up belief in matter, mind and personality—renunciation of that which is already nothing.

What is the meaning of the word *Absolute?* We really cannot define spiritual things in material terms. The best we can say is that Absolute Truth represents that which is eternal, indestructible, glorious and satisfying. It is that *Isness,* unutterable and undefinable.

Labor not with your minds to reach heaven, for the way is a laborless pathway. There is but one door: *Believe that ye are already there.* The Master calls you today. Come; open your vision to the glory of yourself as you eternally *are,* the glory of the kingdom within and at hand.

The point of consideration is not a matter of our goodness or badness, patience or resistance, but it is: Where is my belief? What is my attitude toward Self and Reality?

One can never be held in bondage after he sees its nothingness. As soon as a lie is seen to be a lie, it has no power.

The science of right thinking and right conduct entails strenuous labor. Let us remember the divine decree: "The righteousness of the righteous shall not save him, nor the wickedness of the wicked destroy him." There is no personal goodness or badness. There is no personality at all. The only power is the Truth which one is. The Self is power because of Its own existence. Life is Its own power.

The inspiration and illumination possessing us and manifesting under our praise and recognition of the one Being, *Infinity*, deliver to us instruction not read in books nor heard on hilltops. When one performs miracles, it is as though he stood in a place where he is absent both from the body and from the mind. He is not consciously thinking, yet he is bathed in a blazing light of power, glory and understanding. He does not question whether a certain healing will take place or a certain pocketbook be filled, but he simply looks at Truth and knows the answer.

And what is our guide? What is our standard of knowledge? How shall we determine whether a thing is or is not? Whatsoever things are lovely, whatsoever things bring peace, joy and glory, whatsoever things bring satisfaction and contentment, such have their foundation in Truth.

Why is it more difficult for some to understand Absolute Science than it is for others? Understanding is not a mental function. Understanding is spiritual consciousness. Many are trying to work out their problems of life with their minds as they would do sums in arithmetic. Many have spent years in the study of truth yet have not fulfilled the desires of their hearts, because they have tried to mentally acquire truth instead of to spiritually understand it.

Some there are who read truth or who listen to instruction and immediately believe and accept without question, without argument. It is all settled with them from the start. They *feel* that it is true. Others hear, but they must consider it first; they must debate about it and test it.

Now, he who would prove truth before accepting it has the cart before the horse. If it were a fact that man can actually change from sickness to health, from one stage or condition to another better state by following certain methods and procedures set forth, then he could with impunity seek to prove truth before accepting it. But such is not the case. Man is not to put on health and harmony. Man is not to create it or unfold it or attain it. But man is to believe that he *is* the likeness of God—like God—perfect, changeless, eternal, glorious *now and here*.

Simple, trusting hearts find it easy, joyous to believe in Truth. They do not ask for proof. They know in their hearts, "It is so." They do not argue or strive to reason in their minds just how Truth works and how treatments heal. Their faith is enough to encourage them until fuller understanding is revealed to them, while those who insist upon understanding Truth with their reason find the journey long and wearisome.

Now, one person may read a book that contains wonderful spiritual understanding, a new and fuller presentation of Truth, and still it may make no impression upon him at all. Perhaps he may even think it something very ordinary that he is reading, something commonplace and not at all inspirational.

Another person picks up the same book, and as he reads it is as though someone took him by the hand and led him out into green pastures, where he drank of cool, clear water until he was filled with ecstasy and delight. He is drinking from the well of understanding where everything is shining, bright about him, and now his vision is like crystal. He not only sees and feels Truth, but even more than this—*he is Truth.*

The wonder and glory of such moments, when the act of Truth is at hand, only such as have seen and felt can really understand.

Now, why do not all students of Truth receive the same good from the same book? Because of their different attitudes, their apparently different states of consciousness. One may read a book containing priceless spiritual jewels, yet to him these jewels are of no value, for his own vision is clouded and he recognizes them not.

Another student, having a clear and satisfying understanding of Truth, reads this same book, and while he reads, it is always as though he were on the lookout. He is quick, keen, alert, always watching for new and fuller ideas, and if they are in the book he is sure to find them, to recognize them, to seize them. He has, as it were, within himself a flashlight which blazes on the words, taking from them their essence, their substance, feeding upon them as though he were eating the bread of life and drinking from the living water. The glory of inspiration and revelation is upon him.

O glorious One, how wonderful to behold
Thy presence!
How joyful to be carried away on the
wings of glory and bask in the light of
illumination!
How peaceful, how powerful to recognize
and partake of divine ideas,
Fresh as the breath of morning, fair as the
cloudless day!

It is never too late! Do not look over the past years and grieve because of false steps you have taken, because of precious years you have wasted, because of labors lost. This is only the dream. In heaven there can be no false steps nor any mistakes.

Open your heart and vision to the message of Truth. *There is no time in God!* One day in Truth is the same as a thousand years in a world of attainment. Bravely now, with courage born of insight, look up and cry, "It never happened! I never lost a moment's time! I never made a single mistake! With the vision of God I behold there is no past; there is but the eternal hour of changeless glory and harmony. The moment is here when I perceive clearly the nothingness of experience."

A young man went to his teacher with this question: "Using Absolute Science, how shall I treat so that I can find my right place in business?"

This man was then earning a very small salary and was earnestly desirous of obtaining a better position. The teacher said to him, "Go home and declare that you are in your right place now, that man is always in his right place of abundance and harmony."

He understood and closely followed directions, returning in a few days to relate that he had been called to a position of high order which completely satisfied him at that time.

Now, suppose that this man had stopped to reason and debate over the directions of the practitioner. Supposing that he had thought to himself like this, "Now, how can I say that I am in my right place, when I know it is not true, for I want to make a change? Before I believe in this Science I want to see the proof. When I have a good position offered to me, then I will have some faith and belief." The demonstration would not have been forthcoming.

Listen. We do not declare the truth about appearances, about this seeming world, about experience, but *we declare the truth about perfect man, the truth about the perfect world, the truth about reality.*

Man is always in his right place *in heaven*, is he not? Then accept this fact, believe it without doubt or question, and according to your belief and faith in heavenly things, so shall it come to pass, even in your seeming external or earthly world.

A student went to his teacher explaining that he wanted a business position. He was without employment. He was a capable, worthy man and a truth student; still the demonstration was not made, much to his disappointment.

The teacher said to him, "I suppose that you are desiring a good position. You believe that you have none at present, and you expect truth to help you find something satisfactory to you?" The answer was, as the teacher expected, in the affirmative.

"Then this is why your demonstration is delayed," was the verdict. When you feel ill you do not acknowledge this in Science, but you declare that you are *perfect;* so also you need not accept and believe that you have no position now, but you must see and acknowledge that man is never for a single moment separate from abundance, harmony and satisfaction."

The student recognized his mistake at once and proceeded to demonstrate according to Truth, according to that which *is.* Very soon he was called to a very splendid position.

Be not discouraged if you do not receive insight and understanding at once. It has been asked: "Why should we have to read and study truth; why should we learn if we are all things already?"

Instruction is not for the purpose of delivering something to a student which he has not already. The reason why we read about Truth and listen to instruction is because it is that which Soul already knows—we are coming into our own. We love to hear and to perceive that which is our very own, that which is our nature and our being. It stirs us with mystic joy and delight.

For instance, when one adorns himself with some precious jewels or clothes himself in gorgeous raiment, the very first thing he seeks is the mirror. He delights to view himself, to watch the sparkle of the jewels, to note the style of the garment, *to see himself,* does he not?

As man views himself in the mirror for the satisfaction that it brings and not to add anything to himself thereby; so it is that as one reads a book of truth or listens to instruction, he is not really learning anything, *he is but looking into the mirror of Life and viewing himself as he is.*

"Beloved, *now* are we the sons of God, and it doth not yet appear (to us in this world) what we shall be (in our perfect state); but we know that when he (the real Self) shall appear, we shall be like him, for we shall see him as he is." As the Self looks into the mirror of true instruction, he sees his true likeness: himself *as he is.*

Oh how swiftly love and peace enfold us on the thrill of our recognition of the one Being—Infinity! As flame lights flame, so inspiration fires inspiration, and he who speaks the living Word fans into being that flame in another, for the other is after all, *himself.*

"Inasmuch as ye have done it unto these, ye have done it unto me." How thirstily one drinks as his lips touch the living water, and how hungrily one partakes of supernal bread!

As the day of enlightenment, the day of insight, the day of wisdom sheds its dawning light into the hearts of men so the shadowy night of ignorance is dispelled.

The voice of Light is forever proclaiming:

I speak truth! *I* proclaim that which is eternally true in the consciousness of the one Being! There is no darkness, there is no evil! There is no deception, there is no bondage! There is no dream, there is no sleep! *I* am the Joy of the world. *I* am the Light shining immaculate and supreme! *I* am Authority, Power, Majesty, Glory! *I* am the one and only Presence and Being!

With explanations and illuminations as presented by Absolute Science, the nothingness of sickness, of evil, is made plain. Now, the only sickness that one can ever have is his thought that he is sick. No man can ever be sick actually. He can be sick only in belief. One may ask, "Well, what is the difference? The pain is the same in either case. What does it matter whether one dies in belief or dies actually?"

If one were actually sick, he would never recover. If one actually died, he would remain dead eternally. If one is sick in belief only, then he can be healed in belief, and he can then enjoy the health which he is.

Now, let us see this clearly, that there is no limitation, trouble, evil of any kind except in thought, in belief. All there is to a man's sickness is his thought of it, his belief in it. There is no such thing as evil or limitation except what we think is evil or limitation. We experience sickness, evil, according to our thinking, according to our belief in them, hence they are mental, unreal, and not material or real.

Suppose that you sit at a table to eat some bread, but as you take the slice in your hand preparatory to placing it into your mouth, someone across the table from you hypnotizes you into the belief that it is not bread that you are holding in your hand, but it is a slice of watermelon. So now you take a fork and try to extricate the seeds, and you cut the bread, thinking it is melon. *Is what you eat melon or is it bread?* It is melon to you in this spell, or hypnosis, but you are actually eating bread.

You see, you do one thing in your mind, an unreal, impossible thing, and you do another thing *actually,* of which you are not consciously aware. There is no melon present except in your belief or thought, and eating melon in belief is the same as not eating melon at all. Is it not?

Right here is the place for one to behold clearly as never before that the *thought* of evil, the *thought* of sickness, of poverty, does not make evil, sickness, poverty. Your thought of sickness does not make you sick, for all the time you are perfect and well, but your thought or belief in sickness produces a spell, a mesmerism, so that in belief you are sick, and as soon as you can perceive that the sickness is wholly a mental state, you can then surely behold its nothingness.

There must be belief in sickness in order to experience sickness, and even when one says that he is experiencing it, it is not an actual experience but is an experience taking place in his mind only. Thus, this is why it came about that it has been taught, "Thinking makes it so." Thinking makes it so to you, *to your belief,* but thinking a thing does not actually make that thing.

Thinking the bread is melon does not make it so, does not make the bread melon. Thinking the world evil, the body sick, does not make an evil world nor a sick body except to one in his belief or mental state, which is the very same as not at all.

One may think good thoughts all day long, and still this will not make him good if he is not good already. The same as if while believing that you were eating melon you began to declare that it was really bread, your declaration or right thoughts about it would not make it so, for it would be "so" already. But your *recognition* that it was bread and not melon would dislodge the false belief, and then your right thinking would be an outflow of your right understanding.

Therefore, let us think we are good because we *are* good! Let us think we are well because we *are* well! Let us think we are wealthy and prosperous because we *are* wealthy and prosperous! Let us think we are birthless and deathless because we *are* birthless and deathless! Let us think there is only the One because there *is* only the One!

In plain words, let us not think a thing is true because we wish it that way, but let us declare and assert it is that way because it *is* that way. We are not well and strong and happy and harmonious because of our right statements that we are this way, but it is because we *are* this way—because we are well and happy and strong and prosperous, that we state that we are.

This brings the vision *in* instead of out. This glorifies God on earth as in heaven. This glorifies, recognizes Truth outwardly because it is so *inwardly.* The way of insight is a path over which the feet do not walk nor does the mind travel. It is a way seen only with the divine or incorporeal eye.

Let us know and acknowledge that we are as perfect and as immortal now, *this instant,* as we ever shall be.

One who looked toward the heights boldly wrote: "Stop talking about God and His idea and speak unto majestic Deity face to face! So shall majestic man arise, victoriously daring!"

To be charged to overflow with irresistible miracle-working Spirit while yet in the flesh; to be the radiance of buoyant joy while yet walking among the sons of man; to shed perfume of healing and strengthening and illuminating while yet speaking with us and smiling upon us—this is the final Christian ministry; this is the bloom of full obedience to the sacred edict, *Look unto Me.*

CHAPTER VI

Demonstration

"The crooked shall be made straight," for they are straight *already*. The sick shall be healed, for "before they call" they are answered *already*. Those who ask "shall receive," for no one can ask for any good thing which is not at hand *already*.

It is asked, "Where does illusion end and reality begin?" All beliefs involving rightness and wrongness, goodness and badness, comparisons and opposites are unreal.

When healing is revealed to us as being present, it seems that the illness ends and the reality appears, but the reality was there all the time, even when the illusion of disease seemed to be present. Right in the midst of the greatest problem is that problem's annihilation, is that problem's extinction — *is that problem's nonexistence.* Right in the place where illusion holds sway is Truth — victorious, alone, supreme, mighty, All.

Harmony, beauty, love; unspoilable, unchangeable and immortal goodness, life and intelligence constitute perfect man, the God-being.

Eternal man is never in a mortal world, never in a world of illusion, but is always at the standpoint of understanding, always knowing the allness of Truth and the nothingness of a so-called material or dream world and always experiencing that understanding.

The perfect universe is the expression of divine Mind and divine ideas. Anything that we see in this world which shows forth beauty and harmony and delivers joy and satisfaction has its substance in Truth, and is forever existent, is forever Life expressed as Life. But anything in this world that is not good and lovely, we may be sure has no life, no reality, no substance back of it and so is purely delusion, deception, purely nonexistent.

Everything that is real and true, that is good and desirable, is what is called in the Bible "the creation of God," and is not a mental or dream creation but is the actual, true universe. This "creation" of God is not originated but is the eternal identity of Spirit. It is not the way one looks at a thing that makes it the way it is, for the way it *is* is immovable.

One may dream at night of using a telephone, for instance; may take the instrument in his hand to use it; and to him it may seem broken or out of order, yet he is not actually using the instrument but is using only a *symbol* of it, *using his belief of it,* for the actual telephone does not exist in the dream world in which he is in belief, but exists in this world.

Likewise, when we look at trees and flowers, sun, stars and ocean in this world, if we see falling leaves and dying flowers, if we see an ocean that tortures and kills, we may be sure that we are not seeing Life face to face, but we are seeing as if in a dream, as if through a mist or veil. We are not seeing the ocean as it actually is in the perfect world, but we are seeing a symbol of this ocean as in a dream. We are seeing our belief of it.

The beauty and joy of the ocean, flowers and trees are real and true, but the changing, the hurting, the discordant conditions that we seem to see are not true, but are altogether deception, illusion.

When one feels that he is seeing sickness, sorrow, accident or trouble, let him take his vision away from the deception, from the picture of evil, and turn directly to the true world, the world of reality, and with love and devotion, with quickening Spirit, let him declare what is true in the world of Reality, what he knows exists in the spiritual world; then when he turns his vision again to this world, the deception has gone, the trouble has vanished, and there before him is *the act of Truth.*

In order to bring before your vision in this world any harmony that you desire, you must first of all understand that such action, such harmony has already taken place in the true world. For instance, there may not be houses and offices, cars and clothing in heaven, yet all such things symbolize or dramatize abundance, joy, satisfaction in the spiritual world, and because of the reality of joy and peace in heaven, it is right that we have delivered to us in this seeming world their perfect symbols.

When you wish health instead of sickness, you do not have to move the sickness out of the mind or body; you do not have to do anything at all about it. The same as in the morning when you have been dreaming the night before of traveling in an aeroplane, you do not find this plane in your room when you waken, do you?

You do not have to have the plane extracted from your mind nor from the room, for it has never been present and is wholly imaginary. Its coming, its going, is the very same as nothing at all. Is this not true?

There must come for us that experience which Jesus mentioned as being *in* this world, apparently, yet not being *of* this world. That is, we will be seen and known in this world, we will eat and sleep and wear clothing, but at the same time we will know in our hearts that this is drama, dream only, and therefore entirely harmless.

Man in heaven is constantly feeding upon Truth, the staff of Life, and this reality is expressed or symbolized in the human experience as man partaking of material bread to sustain his physical existence. Now, if man in the human experience, suffering because of certain foods he has eaten, will turn to the spiritual world of spiritual ideas and know that in reality man is forever sustained by Truth, true ideas of which vegetables, bread, etc., are but symbols, and if he will believe the promise, *None of these symbols in a drama world can harm you, for there is no harm in them,* he will find his suffering gone, for he has had a glimpse of heaven.

In the final analysis, we do not have to leave this earth, for we are not really in it. We are therefore not to leave earth for heaven, as has been the popular belief for ages past, but we are to understand the word: Thy kingdom come on earth. The kingdom of Truth is to be recognized as here on earth, for, "The earth shall be filled with the knowledge of the Lord, as the waters cover the sea."

The earth of birth, change, sickness, sin and death shall disappear in belief and instead shall be seen and known the heaven which is here, actually at hand, and in which we are now actually living.

While we are still on earth, in belief, there will come for us the illumination that we are in the kingdom of heaven.

The practice of healing is not an art, nor is healing dependent upon one's spirituality. There is nothing to be done by one to cause him to be more spiritual. *One does not have to do anything to be what he is.* But man is to see the nothingness of personality, personal goodness or personal badness and is to see himself as he *is.*

Man is not to be delivered by any means or methods, but man is to be delivered by Truth. The external and the internal means are not sufficient to bring emancipation on earth. There are no means needed to help man, so man should not look for a method of deliverance. Only that which *is* can deliver man. Such is the message of Truth.

Now, students will wander from one teacher to another teacher, from one book to another book, until they reach that teacher or that book which satisfies them, which strips the scales from their eyes; then they continue to study for the joy of it and to feed upon the bread of Life.

We are not asked to bring about our glory and our perfection; we are asked only to acknowledge it. We are not asked to destroy evil, but to perceive that, "Nothing shall by any means hurt you." True instruction is simple. When one finds that instruction is labor, he may be sure that it is not true instruction.

What are the demands of Truth? Does It ask you to be educated in college? Does It require that one dress or eat or pray after a certain fashion? No. Truth demands our love, our faith, our belief, only.

Neither medicine nor metaphysics nor even death can achieve the end of matter, the end of evil. Truth is the only deliverer. *The end of any deception is the perception of its nothingness.* It is not a matter of education or evolution. It is not a matter of rolling up one's sleeves for an attack, for strife and warfare. Rather is it *stillness.*

It is not mental energy nor vigorous denial nor strenuous affirmation. Rather is it insight that delivers the end of the physical body, the end of evil, the end of a material world.

Healing takes place when one has the insight to understand that there is nothing to be done. It is not a question of using Truth, for Truth cannot be used. Mental acrobatics, realizations, are steps on the way, but they are not the goal. It is said that the shortest distance between two points is a straight line. Even this authority can be set aside, transcended, for the shortest distance from man to Truth is for man to *be* Truth.

There is no distance between man and perfection; between man and reality; between man and Truth.

Treatment, the highest practice, is a recognition that there is no distance, no change, no time, no space in Omnipresence. The message of the kingdom is not "how to have," but it is the study of Reality *present.* True instruction removes from one the belief that power is in the body; that power is in the thought; removes from one the belief that he is not perfect now in body as well as in consciousness.

God made man in his image. Body therefore is not flesh but is the expression or likeness of Truth. *Body is Self manifested!* The treatment is:

I acknowledge the one Presence, the one Power, the one Being. I acknowledge that I live in the love, in the faith, in the heart, in the glory of Truth. I acknowledge the nothingness of mistakes, of past failures, of ignorance, of dreams. I acknowledge the mind of Jesus Christ ever-present. I acknowledge that there is no separation, no departure from Truth, no return to harmony; there is no bondage and there is no escape. There is only the one Being—the Being of changeless love and glory.

Now, healing power operates upon that which is already nothing, for of course, it is plainly seen that Truth could not operate upon that which is perfect. We sometimes hear one voicing something like the following: "I know that sickness is false, and I understand Truth clearly enough for the body to manifest it."

Let it be perceived that the rope that may appear as a snake can never be less than the rope, and one would not say, "And the rope must manifest it." Truth is as true and as ever-present in manifestation as in Spirit. The character, man (including the body) is as perfect as God. It is not a process of manifesting. It is manifested!

There is coming a time when man will give no attention to the changing and the rebuilding of his body, but he will know himself as he is. Attainment is a dream, for it is neither lo, today, nor lo, tomorrow, but it is, "Stand ye still and see."

The charm about right instruction is that it comes to one as drinking from a fountain that satisfies, as walking in green pastures amidst exquisite love and peace. Healing, under true instruction, is not a matter of sitting in any certain position of body, nor breathing in any particular fashion, nor praying with any special phraseology, yet such methods may seem to help one in his journey from earth to heaven, which is really no journey at all.

The treatment which delivers Truth, which delivers harmony, freedom, is that treatment which stands upon nothing, but leaps out of one unawares. There is a power in man that acts not because of man's thinking but in spite of it. It is insight. It is *the act of Truth.* Gradually, this truth will reach over this whole earth—that man is like God, that he cannot be sick, that he cannot be sinful, that he cannot die. Then shall we begin to see the real man as he is, and the dream of matter, mind and personality shall be forever passed.

Often when giving treatments, it seems that the Truth responds to one person more than It does to another. Why is it that one can declare the truth and have a demonstration instantly at hand, while another may declare the same thing, the same ideas, and there will be no proof, no demonstration at hand? Is not the word of Truth quick and mighty? And is not the Truth impartial, looking upon one the same as upon another?

Now, all of us have heard of wonderful demonstrations being made following such simple declarations as, "God is Love," or "God is omnipresent," yet one might repeat these very words when in trouble and they would bring about no help at all. Why is this? If Truth is changeless, and if the Self of one is the Self of all, then why are not results the same in all instances when words of truth are expressed?

Let one who has faith, belief or understanding speak the Word, and let his eyes be closed to externals, closed to that untrue manifestation which seems before his vision, and let him speak the word, "God is the only power," or "God is omnipresent" as though these words were rushing out of him like devouring flame, like some living thing, and lo, the healing takes place; Truth is fulfilled.

Another, while speaking the same words, the same sentences, has his mind fixed on the external world around him; he is speaking to bring about some result; he uses the words as though they were knives to cut. He says, "I will believe in Truth when I see results, and when I am healed, then shall I go about to heal others."

Such ignorance is like seeing Truth through a veil or like running with the feet in shackles, and such is not the *living* Word but is a dead formula delivering no joy, no freedom, no glory.

Here the Word has been used to accomplish something, used with the notion of changing and correcting something. This one believes in time, in cause and effect. He uses the words as *his* words rather than as *the Word.* He uses the words with an idea of accomplishment.

When one utters right words yet places upon them his own conception, when one uses the right speech yet his vision is to the material world, the mental law, the notion of personality, his words have no life in them. When one speaks the Word because it comes out of him rather than comes into him, then the words are alive; then his desire is fulfilled, because such words are Truth.

Many are the testimonies given publicly in churches detailing one's fears, pains and delays, and even though such testimony finally ends with a recital of deliverance, the main fact, the paramount event, should always be that one has come face to face with Truth, that one has heard the Voice, has walked with the Presence, and the dream, the darkness should not be described or pictured but should quickly be dropped from the mind.

There is a health, a body, a world that transcends one's highest ideas and imaginations and is not a creation leaping from any mental activity. Lo, this health, this body, this world is prepared, it is at hand, shining, white, transparent.

Take away the belief that man is asleep, is dreaming, is in a delusion, is in a false world, is in a mortal body, is separate from God, and here stands man in all his wondrous glory in the measure of the fullness of Christ!

Let us behold that we are neither young nor old, that we are neither asleep nor awake from sleep, that we are not in a body nor out of a body, but that we are That which *is*. Let us behold the One as *all* there is.

We note that the blossoms on the trees need sun, heat, moisture, to transmute them into ripened fruit, and so it seems that teachers, books, instruction act upon the minds of individuals similarly. Students submit to rules and laws of teachers and organizations until that hour strikes for them when they perceive the *oneness* of Being and the nothingness of personality. Thereafter, man is not like unripened fruit, but he listens to sermons and to instructions for the joy of it, for the ecstasy and the glory of it.

The man of insight will obey no law of teacher, church or organization; he will not be fettered or bound; he will not be shackled by the notion of any authorization; he will have nothing imposed upon his liberty and freedom.

As children finally leave dolls and toys for higher delights, so man finally feels the living fire within delivering to him the consciousness of the nothingness of personality and the allness of the One.

There is no reproach whatever to be placed upon churches, societies, sermons, teachers, for they all serve as helps on the way, but once the Light breaks and bursts and the heart feels the descent of the Holy Ghost, feels the illumination stripping the veil from off the eyes, lifting the yoke from off the shoulders, thereafter one is an illumined being and rejoices only in the One and admits no other.

One in the Light walks in a different world from one in ignorance, although they breathe the same air and walk on the same sidewalk. Man who places himself under the thoughts and ideas of another is not beholding the one Being, and man who places another beneath himself as subservient in any way to his thoughts and ideas has a still larger vision to express.

Always bring your heart to Truth; always bring your love. Say often, "I love the Truth. I love everyone, for I see none separate from the One." We will come to the hour when we do not speak truth for demonstration, but speak it because we love to speak it. Does not the promise read "Because he hath set *his love* upon me, therefore shall I deliver him"?

To see that healing is as much a belief as is sickness is insight, and insight is Truth knowing Itself, or is Self-consciousness.

As man asleep is exiled from his room and his surroundings because of the ignorance of his mind, because of the cutting off of his senses, so ignorance of Life, of Truth, of the one and only Being causes us to be exiled from the spiritual world—not actually, but mentally.

The man asleep on the couch has his watch ticking under his pillow, but he is utterly unconscious of it. His hands are resting upon the bedspread, but he feels it not. The picture on the walls, the furniture in the room are directly before his vision, yet unseen, unknown to him.

Is not this clear and compelling illustration showing us that if we can be in this so-called material world and know it not, and neither feel, see, nor hear what is directly at our elbow, we must admit the possibility of being in a heavenly world, not seeing, feeling or being conscious of these heavenly things about us.

As man is never actually in any dream at night but is always on the couch, so man never actually lives in any material world, in any world of birth, change and death, but is always happy and harmonious in the world that manifests Truth.

Now, it seems to us that we arrive by learning and that we are continually adding to our store of understanding by reading books and hearing instruction, does it not? This is not so, however, for the truth is that we are always conscious of what we know.

When one believes in a delusion, he does not know it to be a delusion, does he? He must see the truth before he knows a delusion to be delusion. Before you understand the nothingness of personality, you cannot see that all men are one being. This is why the truth makes us free, for as soon as one knows the truth, then the illusion vanishes.

Let us not only know that there is truth, but let us know what this truth is. A man might die of hunger in this world, even though he had in his pocket a roll of bills, unless he knew this. Of what use would the money be in his pocket if he did not know it was there?

Is it not the same with man who does not know who or what he is? Will he not go on being sick, while all the time he is a changeless being? Will he not go on dying, while all the time he is an immortal being?

As man has estimated himself to be other than he is, he will therefore waken from this delusion or see this delusion to be delusion when he receives Truth.

We read of the man wandering off from his wealthy home and eating husks, but there arrived that moment when he came to himself. And so there is always this time for us all, this time when we "come to ourselves." It may be in an hour of deepest darkness; it may be in an hour of purest delight; but whatever the hour when the veil is removed, the fact remains that the kingdom of heaven is already at hand and we are already in it.

"If I make my bed in hell, behold, Thou art there!" Truth sees the good and the bad alike; sees hell and heaven the same, for Truth is not double-minded but sees oneness, sees Itself and Its kingdom as *all* there is.

There is no hell in Truth and no truth in hell. There is no hell at all; there is only God.

Man can think he is in hell, can think he is sick, can even think he is dead; still his thought cannot change or interfere with the fact that he is always experiencing the kingdom of heaven.

Now, how can one who is in the kingdom know and feel and experience that kingdom? Except ye be converted! Except ye be born again! Except ye give up your life!

Nothing that we can do, think or say will cause us to be any place other than where we are in the kingdom. This is wonderful insight that opens to one the pearly gates of heaven. *Nothing that I can do, think or say can cause me to be other than I actually am!*

"*Act* as though *I* were, and ye shall know *I am.*" One says, "But how can I rise and walk when I am crippled and weak? How can I eat a hearty meal when I cannot retain even a baby's diet? How can I do the things that I would love to do when my body, mind and Soul seem shackled, bound?"

Listen. No disease in all this world ever held or bound a man. It is *belief* in disease but not disease that binds and holds man in chains and slavery. And as long as one "treats" pain and disease, he is believing in it, is he not? And if he would disbelieve in it, he would come forth; he would rise and walk.

A young woman was thought to be in a very serious illness. She had not eaten nor slept for several days, and although she was an earnest truth student, her demonstration had not been made. The practitioner who was assisting her said to her at this time, "If you did not believe that you were ill, what would you be doing now?"

"Oh, I should be dressing for an urgent engagement that I have tonight."

"Well, since you know the truth, which is that you are in heaven now, acting as it pleases you, why not *act out* this truth now? Why not lay aside entirely, like closing a book, the belief that you are weak and ill and act out what you know is true in heaven?"

The student saw the point, caught the vision. "I will," she cried.

Somehow she managed to rise from the bed, and there were those who lovingly helped her to dress. She was seated before a mirror and someone was arranging her hair when it was noticed that her head drooped and fell. It was discovered that she was sound asleep!

Gently, swiftly, she was undressed and carried back to bed, where she slept soundly until the following morning when she wakened as fresh as the lark, as happy as the glorious day.

When we see that we are feeding upon husks—sickness, sorrow, trouble—and we turn with our love toward that Light, to those everlasting arms that ever await us, have we not found that, "But when he was a great way off his father saw him and had compassion and ran and fell on his neck and kissed him."

Is it not, after all, a little thing to do—*only believe?* Peter's heart was heavy until he felt the Master's hand warmly, firmly, grasping his, then triumphantly, victoriously, he walked on the waves. Peter saw, he felt the living Savior, and it was a simple matter for him to believe. But we read in the Book of Life, "Blessed are they that have not seen and yet have believed."

We must have faith enough to believe in the Unseen. We must feel the invisible Presence the very same as though It were visibly before us— then It is visibly before us.

Believing in the everlasting arms, we can actually feel them. Believing in the Presence, in the Power, in the Love divine as here and now, we can actually hear the Voice, feel the Touch and see the Form, divine.

CHAPTER VII

Questions and Answers

Many students have certain specific questions they would like answered, and we shall now take up some of these queries and explanations, as doubtless they will be of deep concern to many readers.

"I cannot understand how mind or mentality is nothing, yet creates. How can nothing create something?"

It can be easily seen that the mind that creates worlds, people, animals, houses, sun, moon and earth in the night dream is experiencing a false creation and that both the mind and its creation are nothing. The mentality does not create something, but creates pictures, illusions, deceptions— *nothing,* whether in the night dream or in the dream of material existence.

One of clear spiritual vision wrote: "Mortal mind creates its own physical conditions ... You must instruct mortal mind with immortal Truth."

Now, mortal mind, or the human mentality, is not true Consciousness, and therefore all that it creates is like a dream creation, having beginning and end. One might easily challenge, "How, absurd, how unscientific for anyone to proclaim that we must "instruct mortal mind with immortal Truth," for the same author wrote elsewhere, "'Scientifically speaking, there is no mortal mind'."

Many of us have found that much mental confusion can be avoided if we will, first of all, determine whether the author is speaking absolutely, from the plane of Reality, or speaking relatively, from the plane of the human experience. We find apparent contradictions throughout the Bible and in most books on Mind or Truth, but such contradictions vanish under the light of *insight* or understanding of the author's platform.

When it is written that mortal mind creates its own physical conditions, such a statement concerns the human experience. Mortal mind (wrong thinking and believing) creates sin, sickness, death, yet such creation is nothing actual, nothing that has God, Truth, back of it; therefore, such creation is illusion, dream substance only, and when mind is instructed with immortal Truth then such unreal creation ceases.

The question arises, "But how can that which is nothing be taught or instructed?"

We know, do we not, that we cannot instruct Intelligence? We also know that there is no *actual* way from earth to heaven—the only path being that of belief or insight. The way of demonstration, then, is first through belief and later through insight.

Merely declaring, "I am the Truth; I am a perfect being in heaven now," will not deliver to you a heavenly experience, for one must either believe in Truth or understand Truth in order to experience heavenly harmony.

Teaching or instructing the mind is therefore a device, the same as any belief is a device. The only reason why understanding takes place at all is because man already knows and understands all things.

The real reason why Jesus or any one understanding Truth carries on instruction is, "This is for the glory of God." Those who know Truth know that when they heal or instruct, they do not heal or instruct, but that all things are done for the glory of God, the glory of Truth.

Suppose that a child enters a dimly lighted room and screams with terror because there in the corner of the room is a dark, peculiar looking object. Now, his mother, entering the room, knows the truth, that is, she knows that a fur-trimmed cloak is thrown in such a manner over a chair as to give the appearance of some unknown animal.

Shall this mother instruct the *true* mind of her child? No. Intelligence, true Mind cannot be instructed, nor can it be deceived. Since the child believes that a fearful object is in the room and since his true Mind does not need to be instructed, then it must be "mortal mind" or a *false sense of mind* that needs instruction, must it not? The mother could not move the animal out of the room, for it is not present, showing that there is no *actual* way of deliverance for this child.

The path, therefore, is either through belief or through understanding. The mother might pick up the cloak and thrust it into a cloak closet. The child then would be quieted, soothed through *belief*—belief that the fearful object could no longer harm. Or, the mother could swiftly bring understanding to the child by turning on the light, exposing the presence of the fur-trimmed cloak.

Again, when one attends college, studying astronomy, art, languages, it is not Intelligence, true Mind, that is instructed, is it? And if one commits some sin, we surely do not consider healing or instructing the true Mind, which Jesus said could not sin, do we? "Who convinceth me of sin" was his daring challenge.

When one is sick, in pain or distress, we do not administer help to divine Mind, do we? Thus we are brought face to face with the fact that since it is not divine Mind which is instructed, helped, healed, *it must be mortal mind or the human mentality.*

Such instruction, such healing, however, is like nothing at all happening or taking place, for human existence, existence in the flesh, existence in a changeable world is itself but deception, illusion, dream.

When mortal mind is instructed, it is not an actual process, for such instruction is a device only, displacing false sense with truth. False mind cannot actually be taught but can be coalesced into nothingness, thus revealing the allness and infinitude of Intelligence.

If you were dreaming that you were walking over a long stretch of country road and someone in a car stopped and invited you to ride, you would feel in your dream that it would be much pleasanter to travel over this long stony road via automobile than to walk that same distance, would you not?

Now, the one standing in the road and entering the automobile symbolizes *mortal man*, and the mind considering the walk and the road and the car symbolizes *mortal mind*, for it was none other than this mind that created the road and the car and created the one standing there. But this mind, if told, if instructed, "*You are not here in this road at all; you are but dreaming this,*" would cease its dream, would cease itself, and the whole dream of nothing would vanish.

Suppose that one is a practitioner, a healer and teacher, but finds that his office is empty. Whereas he would heal, there are no sick arriving; whereas he would preach, there are no students seeking his instruction. How then is he to demonstrate? How is he to instruct his mind about this problem?

He is to tell his mind that there are no sick people, that there are none to be taught, and that he, the true man, knows that immortals are always drinking with him of the river of the water of Life, are always partaking with him of the joys of true instruction. Such "instruction" then would be no actual instruction, but would dislodge this false belief, this false mind, to the glory of Truth.

As these lines are being written, a letter arrives with this question: "Do you claim that the body that we see is mortal, or is the body spiritual as long as one is thinking rightly?"

In the dream of human experience, as well as in the sleeping dream, the dreamer thinks that his body is material, that it has sensation, life. Now, one's body is as material to him as is his belief. In the dream of material living the body is controlled by the mind, but *in reality* Soul governs the body, for the true body is the reflection of Spirit, Soul, Self.

We do not have to develop or unfold or attain a perfect body, for the body was, is and ever shall be perfect. The image of Spirit must be as perfect as Spirit.

Another asks, "Did you not think and reason to write your books?"

Yes. There is no reproach against thinking. One should think and reason. One should not go around with his eyes closed because he discovers that God is his sight. We do not give up our eyes and ears, our hands and feet, nor do we renounce our thought and reason when we learn that matter is nothing, for Truth is all.

A false sense of the mind and of the body is all that we ever have to give up. We keep the eyes, the ears, the hands and feet. We keep the mind and the body. We keep that which brings peace and love and joy and glory.

A mirror is true when it is clear and clean and reflects a true picture. We should think of mind and body as perfectly reflecting Soul, Life, Love.

We use our senses, knowing that they are not material but that they are spiritual, perfect. We do not think of our mind as mortal and false, but we think of Intelligence as divine and as forever reflecting right ideas. We think of our bodies as spiritual, as marvelous as the light of day.

In the night dream the mind believes that it has two bodies, one on the couch and another out in the dream. In the dream of walking over the long stretch of country road and encountering the automobile, it believed that it had a body that stepped into the car and drove away. Now, although the mind thought and experienced such a body, there was only the *one* body all this time — the body on the couch. The other body was a dream body, a belief body, only.

Entirely separate from the dream world is the waking experience. Entirely separate from the waking experience is the *actual* universe.

Entirely separate from the belief that our hands can touch objects only within a radius of an arm's length is the fact that our hands might touch the sky. Entirely separate from the belief that we can see only within the radius of a certain number of miles, we have a vision that can reach over the universe. We have bodies that can be visible and invisible, that can be light as the air, weightless as the feather, brilliant as the sun.

Entirely separate from the belief of a mortal, sick, aging body is the perfect, birthless, deathless body of Light.

When the Universe and Man are interpreted by Science they can be understood, but when one seeks to interpret them from the basis of matter and mind, they continue to be but mystery, enigma.

The idea of living in a false world, a dream world, in a false body, a dream body, is dispelled as one believes, accepts and understands Truth. The day of judgment for us is that day in which we know that we are living in the land of Reality, *now*; that we are drinking now of the living water even as Jesus declared.

One conquers the material world when he sees that there is no material world to conquer. One overcomes matter when he sees that there is no matter to be overcome. One overcomes a lie when he perceives the nothingness of the lie. One heals the sick when he knows the unreality, the nothingness, the deception of sickness. One raises the dead when he knows there are no dead.

One triumphs over mortality as he recognizes the *One Being!* The redemption of the world is: *We are in the land of Truth now!*

At any hour, at any moment, man can walk in the heavenly world, the kingdom of Truth, according to his vision, according to his understanding. Nothing is impossible to him who believeth.

Demonstrations over the body are not made when one moves away from the body, nor when one endeavors to separate himself from his body, but *demonstrations are made when one forgets his body*. Miracles take place when one forgets his hands and feet, forgets his thoughts and meditations, when something snatches him up and away, and all he knows is that he is the joy of Truth.

I recall an early experience which I was never able to explain materially. It happened while dressing one morning that I discovered that the heel of one of my shoes was completely missing, and at that time I had no other available pair. This was a great catastrophe to me, as my feet were causing me much suffering, and these were the only shoes that I could manage to wear; besides, at this time I was leaving the house early for the business world.

I immediately telephoned a practitioner, stating the seeming condition to her. I explained that I had a brand new pair of shoes in my closet, but they were too small for me to wear comfortably, as I was suffering very much with swollen, tender feet. She advised me to wear them, nevertheless, saying that although to the world it seems that a quart could not be placed into a pint measure, still it *could* be done, and finished her advice with the Bible command: "Stand therefore, having ... your feet shod with the preparation of the gospel of peace."

Now, I had never doubted Truth, nor the Bible promises, nor my practitioner's understanding, and obedience always came very easy to me. It never occurred to me at this time to do other than

I was told to do. Accordingly, I brought out the new, tight shoes from the closet, shoes which I had never worn, and I shoved and pushed my feet into them, lacing them tightly to the top, while all the time the tears came splashing down my cheeks for ·my suffering seemed very great.

There were two long flights of stairs to be encountered. I took a few steps but it was impossible for me to proceed, as the pain was now overpowering. I then decided to sit on the steps one at a time. In this fashion, I finally reached the main floor.

Just at this moment I saw our letter carrier entering the vestibule, and as I did not want him to see me in this position, I took hold of the post near me for support, hiding behind it until he went out and off the porch. Then something took place which only those who believe in miracles will accept: *I never knew how I left that position, how I traveled a mile to my place of position!*

The next time that I became conscious of my body was late that afternoon. Sitting alone at my desk, my glance happened to fall down upon my shoes. I couldn't seem to place or recognize them. Why, where, what—then, like a flash it came sweeping over me. *My feet!*

Stunned, I sat in the chair, traveling back in my mind to the moment when I hid behind the post, but I could go no further. How I left my home, how I traveled to a place a mile away was a complete mystery to me. And I have never known.

So completely had I lived apart from my body all this time that it was as though I had no body, no feet at all. I now discovered that the shoes were perfectly comfortable, and that night when I glanced at my feet, I found that they were quite normal, and all the discordant conditions had vanished.

In an hour when ye think not, you will find yourself in heaven. Take ye no thought! There must arrive that hour when man *forgets* that he is sick, when man *forgets* that he is in pain, when man *forgets* that he is in prison, when man *forgets* that he is in a material world.

O how glorious to forget matter, to forget mind, to forget personality. How marvelous to forget to prepare food to sustain life, to forget to sleep, to forget to labor with hands and minds.

And there shall be no more death, neither sorrow nor crying, neither shall there be any more pain; for the former things are passed away.

Forgetting the dream, we waken to the real. Forgetting the untrue we find only the true. Forgetting the evil, we perceive the glory. Forgetting the many, we perceive the *One!*

One day a man lay in a dying state. He could not move hand nor foot. He sent for a practitioner, who came and seated herself at his side. They were both silent for several moments. Then it came to the practitioner what a queer idea of man this was. Why, he couldn't move, he couldn't walk, he couldn't talk. How did he compare with God's man of glory and light and marvel and wonder? O, what a mockery, what a parody!

Suddenly it came to her that it was like a joke, a big joke. She actually felt like laughing. Soon, the man on the bed moved his face and looked at her and smiled. Soon they both smiled. Then they commenced to laugh together, quietly at first, then noisily and heartily.

"Why, I can't stop laughing," he said. He caught the vision. "Do you think I could move—could sit up—could stand?" he whispered.

"Why not?" laughed the one at his side. And this man on the bed forgot his pain, forgot to die, for in the twinkling of an eye he had understood; he had seen the farce; he had seen through the veil. No longer deceived, he walked forth as he *was*, the whole, glorious man of God.

"How can one stop an illusion?" it is asked. "For instance, if one is deluded into believing that he has sickness, how can he cease such delusion?"

What destroys error is disbelief in it. One never treats matter or mind or body or personality. What one does is to know and declare and insist that a belief has no effect upon the mind or body, that a belief has no effect upon life, substance or reality.

If one were dreaming at night that he was in a burning building, racing from window to window, from floor to floor for a way of escape, how can the building, the fire and the notion that he is in danger be compelled to cease? *Shut off the dream.* If the dream stopped, then the man in the burning building, the fear, the fire would all cease automatically. Is this not so? For the root, the avenue, the channel for this illusion of false pictures is the notion of a dream. To shut off a dream would be to shut off its pictures.

Now, the channel for a false dream in the waking or human experience, the channel for the pictures of pain, fear, disease, evil, is the dream called false belief. This was clearly shown in the example of one who is eating bread yet is believing that he eats melon. If the one who is eating the bread did not have the belief that it was a melon, he would not have that false picture of melon before his vision, would he?

When the people stopped believing the earth to be flat, the false picture of the flat earth which they appeared to see ceased. And what caused the belief that the earth is flat to cease? The perception that the earth is spherical.

Now, in our waking experience, called human existence, the false pictures called disease, evil, can be traced back to *false belief,* and then we must acknowledge that the deliverer of false belief is Truth. When one sees the bread to be bread, then the delusion automatically ceases. When one sees that the earth is round, the delusion that it is flat is set aside. And when one is conscious of the act of Truth, conscious of Understanding, *then the false belief is rendered nil.*

All limitations called evil, sickness, are destroyed automatically as *belief in them* is destroyed, shut off. In the world of reality there is no false belief. There is no false belief in heaven, no false belief in the spiritual world. Therefore, when we treat, we not only perceive the nothingness of the pictures called evil and limitation, but we also perceive the nothingness of the *false belief* or channel through which they seem to come.

Now, it is plain to be seen that the dream at night could not come into play without a dreamer, without a mind to weave it out into dream pictures. It is like this in the dream called material existence, existence in the flesh. If there were no one to believe in evil there would be no false pictures called evil to be seen. Is this clear to you?

A dream could find no channel without a dreamer, and the experience called sickness would find no channel without a believer.

"How can I demonstrate friends, a companion, a home of my own?"

Know that the way you wish to be is the way you *are*. The actuality is first, and the wish is secondary. Without the actuality there would be no wish, the same as without the original there would be no picture of that original. All *things* are possible, for all *things* are but pictures, images.

Today we are here; tomorrow we are there. Let us perceive that the here and the there are the same. The rose in the mirror and the child in the mirror are the same, for neither one is there. The here and the there, the "this" and the "that" are all images in the mind (mirror). One can have one as well as another.

Our companions are the immortals, spiritual beings. We are actually never alone, never weary, never lonesome. We are living in the midst of divine companionship, experiencing the joys, beauties and harmonies of heaven. This is the fact of Truth which we declare because it is so. This recognition is like the act of holding a rose before a mirror. The rose inevitably appears in the mirror. Holding the facts of Life in our vision, we very soon see their reflection in this world about us.

Friends, companions, homes open up to us as though by magic and in such charming and unexpected fashion.

Labor not with affirmations and denials, but toss your wish lightly into the mirror of effulgence, understanding that it is because it is already granted that you can have it; that it is now at hand, that it is already visible before you. It is because of the coming of your wish that the hour is here; the moment has arrived when you are to enjoy the experience of it.

When our bell reverberates in the front hall, this is an announcement to us that someone has come, someone stands waiting admittance. And with our feet in the true road and our vision placed on high, when the wish throbs within us, we can be sure that something awaits us, something is calling our attention; the moment is here when we are to experience some fuller joy, some greater delight.

Thus we perceive that man reaches all things through himself.

"How can I stop thinking wrong thoughts, foolish thoughts, thoughts that I do not wish to think?"

In the first place, do not fight them. You know what happens when you stand before a mirror and throw out your arms and toss your head, do you not? Therefore do not fight thoughts with thoughts. There is a better way.

Instead of seeing and feeling and hearing such thoughts as though they were part of you, speaking to you from within, learn to look upon them as though they were apart *from* you, separate from you, the, same as if one approached you with a story which you did not care to hear, for you were otherwise occupied, and you turned away to be alone. So when these moods or unruly thoughts come upon you, do not be excited or cast down or combative or overwhelmed, but learn to look at them and *turn away from them*, learn to look at them and *understand* them.

Now, once you can perceive their nothingness, you will be surprised the quietness and the calmness that will be with you. When you are afraid of your thoughts, when you would flee from them, you are mesmerized into believing that they are *something*, that they have power, are you not?

With but a grain of understanding or insight you can perceive that there is no power at all in the mind nor in the thoughts of the mind. This insight will afford you immediate relief. You will run no longer in terror of your thoughts, but you will stand still and look at them, the same as you might look at a picture of a lion on a sheet of white paper. It looks as though it might harm, but all the same you know that it *can't.* Look upon thoughts of fear, of doubt, of worry, of hate, of jealousy, as though you were looking upon something apart from yourself, something utterly without power, something that *can't* harm.

Say to these thoughts, if you like, "Go on, fear as much as you like, worry as much as you please; it really doesn't matter to me. Since you are nothing anyhow, it really doesn't matter what you say. As long as you can't *do* anything, or *be* anything, why, it doesn't really matter how you race around or flurry or fume. It really doesn't matter to me at all, for I perceive you are *nothing.*"

And when you say this, you must *feel* it to be so, and presently you will be quite alone; these evil companions which you believed were part of you will have entirely vanished. Always when you wish a thing to cease, to depart, to vanish, to be still, see that thing in its true light; see that thing as *nothing.* To see a thing as nothing is to be delivered from the false belief, and to be delivered from false belief is true deliverance, is emancipation, is the act of Truth.

Look upon moods, mental thoughts as though you were looking at pictures on the wall. You will then be able to control your mind. And as you pierce through this wall of ignorance, you assert the truth about yourself. You look to that which is

Yourself, and you say with love and assurance, "I am happy, I am content, I am free, I am peaceful because of the Truth which is established, because of the Truth which is omnipresent, because of the Truth which is here, now. I do not believe in evil; I do not believe in fear; I do not believe that power is in anything except in Truth, in God Almighty."

Understanding is demonstration. Understanding is power, is freedom. Understanding of the Allness and the nothingness is emancipation, salvation.

Instruction helps one to tear off the garment of ignorance, helps one to cease believing falsely about himself. Instruction comes to the thirsty one like a flask of pure, cold water. Instruction comes to the fearful one like gentle benediction, like an angel presence, like a garment of peace thrown around one, like loving arms enfolding one. Instruction comes to the ignorant one like beautiful music in his ears, like new paths for his feet to walk upon, like a new world which he is entering. Instruction comes to the hungry heart like *living fires* blazing and burning, bearing him up on wings of Love divine, delivering to him a glory unspeakable, a peace, a glory, a power indescribable.

CHAPTER VIII

Science and Wealth

How are we to find happiness in this world? How can we have the things that we would love to have? These are the questions that are continually being asked.

Well, if one can see how the dreamer can have things in his night dream by turning to *this* world, by remembering what he has in his waking experience, he will also be able to see how it is that one can have such things as he desires in this world by turning his mind to what he actually has *in heaven*.

For example: A man is dreaming that he is very poor, so poor that he hasn't a penny to keep him from starvation, so weary that he sits in poverty and despair. Suddenly, in the dream, he remembers this world and his daily experience; he recollects going to the bank and cashing a check for fifty dollars. Then, in great joy, in his dream he puts his hand to his hip pocket, draws out his wallet and there is the fifty-dollar bill to meet all his needs!

Now, bear in mind that the fifty-dollar bill all this time remains in the wallet which is resting under his pillow. He really does not touch this bill at all, but what he is using in his dream, spending for clothes and food, is picture money—a dream substance, a *symbol* of that fifty-dollar bill that rests under his pillow—but all the same, sufficient to satisfy his dream!

Again, we will assume that one is dreaming that he intends to start on a long journey. His bags are packed and waiting on the porch. He dreads this long journey which he is going to take on foot and expects that he will be weary and tired and that the bags will be very heavy.

Suppose that in his hour of need he recollects *this* world and his experience in *this* world. Then he exclaims, "Since I have a car in the garage, why should I undertake this journey by foot?" Then in his dream, he hurries to the garage, takes a key from his pocket and unlocks the car. He starts the motor running, tucks in the bags and off he goes traveling in peace and comfort.

If one can perceive the value of remembering the waking state while in the night dream, surely one is then in a position to perceive the mystic value of Jesus' words, "Believe that ye have (in heaven) and ye shall receive (on earth)."

When the man in the night dream remembered that in his waking state he had a fifty-dollar bill, he then received the fifty-dollar bill in his dream state, did he not? Therefore, if man in this world, in what is called the state of human experience, will turn to heaven, will remember, will believe what is actually his in heaven, he will then receive in this world.

We have been told that we already have every wish fulfilled in the spiritual world, but what one wishes to know is how to have the things that we desire in *this* world, and it is by understanding the dream and other illustrations that this question of our relation to this world can be understood and abundance and success demonstrated.

In the night dream the man did not actually take his car from the garage, but all the time lay quietly on the bed; yet as long as he used the car in his dream, this was all that was necessary at this time. Is this not so? Nor did he actually take the money from his wallet, but he took the symbol of it, the picture of it, *which was enough.*

Now, in the very same way, we do not receive houses and jewels, food and clothes, money and lands by taking them actually out of the spiritual world and bringing them into this world. It isn't necessary. We can have them in a way that will be the same to us, for a world of birth and change is not an actual world but is a picture world, a symbolic world, a dream-substance world.

Because of the perfection of the spiritual world in which we actually live, it is possible for us to govern our earthly experience harmoniously.

When you wish to place a flower in the mirror, how do you bring this about? How do you get a reflection of a rose? By placing the flower or rose before the mirror. We have then the trinity — the rose outside, the mirror, and the reflection.

In order to have the *reflection* of the rose, an actual rose is placed before the mirror, is turned to the mirror; likewise, in order that we have the *reflection* of wholeness, which reflection is health, we look into the heavenly world; we turn our attention, our vision to reality, heaven, and according to our vision, so is the reflection. Why is this? Because we turn our mind (mirror) to Truth, and then it must of necessity reflect Truth.

For example, if man finds himself in pain in this world, let him turn away entirely from this world and look into heaven, remembering what he actually is in heaven. The same as the dreamer remembered his car and his fifty-dollar bill, so this man in pain in the waking state remembers that man in heaven is perfect, that man in heaven has no pain, that there is no pain in the perfect world. Then the pain is gone and he moves again in peace and harmony.

Believe that ye have in the heavenly world, the world of reality, and you will receive in this world, the mental and physical world of nothingness.

Do we have to leave this world in order to enter heaven? It is not necessary for us to be taken out of a world of sin and evil, for we are not in it. This simplifies the problem indeed, does it not? The man asleep and dreaming has his mind occupied with false pictures, and the man in this world who sees sickness, sin and evil has his mind occupied with false pictures also.

One is never to treat a dream world, for it is useless, and one should never treat dream pictures. Simply announce, acknowledge, recognize the nothingness of a dream and the allness and presence of Truth, the spiritual world, and the darkness disappears in the presence of light; so the dark dream called evil that seems to be in this world disappears in the consciousness of Truth.

The problem of supply is one of the easiest to handle and demonstrate, yet one of the most difficult and delicate of explanation. For this reason it is seldom expounded in books based on the Absolute teaching, although it can be clearly explained in private instruction. As many students are desirous of at least a few helps on this subject, we will try to give these, and those who have the insight, not only to read the lines but also to read "between the lines," that is, to glean the meaning, will find tremendous help from the Absolute teaching on this subject.

The question is asked, "How can I demonstrate money, a home, an automobile?"

Now, you do not believe there are brick houses and hundred-dollar bills and Pierce Arrow cars in heaven, do you? Can you see that they belong to this world only, that they belong to the world of creation? They are called creation for they have a beginning and end.

Now, although creation is transitory and unreal, still it is right to have these things, for did not Jesus say, "Your heavenly Father knoweth that ye have need of all these things"? What things? Food and clothing and the things that make a harmonious experience. But the joy and pleasure of these things consist in understanding their *nothingness.*

As previously expressed, if one in his dream at night realizes he is but dreaming, that he is not in any actual experience, but he is only dealing with *nothing,* he may then have his dream the way he pleases.

Inasmuch as this waking experience, that of being born and laboring for means to live upon this earth is similar to a dream experience, then the consciousness of this fact will enable one to have his dream the way he pleases. If one desires houses, land, money, with the idea that they are something, then he is handicapped from the start, for to deal with nothing (the dream) and think of it as *something* (reality) is to walk in the dark, to live in ignorance, while to deal with nothing as though it were *nothing* is to experience freedom, joy, and the satisfaction of desire.

Since creation springs from nothing, then such nothing is infinite, and one has only to understand *why* he can have his wish granted and the demonstration becomes simple. A demonstration is hard and retarded when one fixes his wish on a thing as if it were *something*, but when he fixes his attention or his wish on a thing as though it were *nothing*, then the demonstration is easy, and at hand.

You can see clearly that in the night dream one can have at once everything he wishes, if he knows that he is the creator of the dream and that it is a dream. But if he doesn't know this, if he doesn't know in his dream that he is dreaming and that all his experience is being made, woven out of nothing, and since the nothing is infinite he can have it as he pleases, then he is deprived of a pleasant dream through ignorance. This should be very plain to one.

A simple illustration or story makes the way of demonstration very clear and simple. A child approaches his mother asking for a story. "Mother, tell me a story, please." The mother, taking the young child upon her lap, after a moment's meditation, begins: "Once upon a time there was a little girl who was very lonesome because she had no pets of any kind to play with. One day there came into her yard one tiny little kitten..."

"Oh, Mother, why can't there come *more* than one little baby kitten?" protests the child.

"Why, yes, of course," assents the mother, continuing, "One day there came *three* little baby kittens into the yard."

Now, the question is, Why could the mother so easily change her story? Why could she say three or five kittens as well as to say one kitten? From what source are these kittens being obtained? *From the nothing.* In the nothing are an infinite number of kittens, as many as this mother could think or say. Is this not so?

This nothing is like a mirror. A mirror is nothing, yet out of a mirror anything can spring. Anything that is before the mirror can be seen also in the mirror as *reflection.* The great nothing from which the kittens have come is similar to the mirror, and the kittens themselves are the reflection, or the image, in the nothing. Both the image in the mirror and the mirror are nothing.

The great nothing, therefore, from which creation springs has been called the mother of creation, for without a mirror you can have no reflection, and without the great nothing there would be no creation.

If one were to draw some pictures on a blackboard, he draws on the nothing. If something were already written on the board, he would not be able to draw or create his pictures. If one wishes to write a book, he writes on blank paper—he writes on the nothing. Then it must be seen that one can have as much of abundance as he pleases because of the infinite Mirror from which it springs.

To illustrate how such demonstrations are made practical, I will give a few of my own in simple language, for they relate to everyday experiences.

Take a shopping trip, for instance. Sometimes one knows just what he wishes to purchase, knows the color, size and cost of the article; yet again, one may not be certain or may have no definite idea at all about the thing that he wishes to have. In either case, a demonstration is possible and easy to be made.

On a shopping trip one day I planned to buy a coat. I did not know this time just what particular kind of a coat I wanted, and I visited several shops but did not find a single thing that I liked. As it was about time for my train, I knew that a demonstration would have to be made at once, or else I would not make the purchase that day.

Seating myself in the shop in which I found myself at this moment and in which the saleslady had shown me everything she had in this line and still nothing that I liked, I closed my eyes for a few moments and it came to me clearly like this: "The coat that I want is in the nothing, or is unknown to me. It is so absolutely nothing and so unknown to me this moment that I haven't even the slightest idea of the color or the style that I would like. Yet, since the nothing holds all creation, it *is* there, it is *here—*"

The saleslady now touched my elbow. "I have found another," she said, smiling. With the glee of a child I reached for it while the voice sang within me, *"This is it."*

Now, the coat which she brought me was *reversible.* No wonder I hadn't planned it! I could wear it on either side. It was delightful, fitted me perfectly, and as in a fairy tale, I bought it and reached my train on time.

Now, here is another instance of demonstration, and this time I knew exactly what I wanted, yet still it seemed difficult at the outset to procure. I wanted a country house where I might spend some peaceful summer hours away from city life. I knew exactly to the minutest detail what I desired.

It must be a white house with green blinds. It must have a sweeping lawn with plenty of maples for shade—a cool, quiet, secluded spot. Yes, and I wanted some water: a lake or a running brook on the place; and this house must be within comfortable motoring distance from my city home.

Now, one does not sit and wait for his desire to fall from the sky, but he acts out what seems reasonable and at hand. I therefore made my want known to several agents who laughed at me and informed me that what I wanted was impossible. "That is just a pleasant little dream you have," they said. But I knew that such a dream could come *true*.

About a week later one of these men took me to see a place which he thought might suit me but which was nothing at all that I had asked for; yet it was while standing here that suddenly he said to me, "Right around the corner is a beautiful place, but the owner prefers to leave it idle rather than rent it. We might look at it."

The moment we came within sight of the place, I recognized it. *"This is it,"* sang within me. Here was the white house with green blinds. Here every wish had been granted me, as though the house were made to order for me. There were eighteen acres of land to this place, and through this and very close to the house ran the bubbling brook; and I counted twelve stately maples standing in the front yard.

Soon I was talking with the owner, explaining to him that I wished to come to this lovely place of peace and seclusion, coolness and fragrance, to write a book. *And it is right here in this demonstrated spot that I am writing these very lines!*

Many students write asking, How can I sell my home? How can I pay my debts? How can I obtain my desires?"

We are to see first of all that we are dealing with *nothing*, dealing with creation, dealing with magic, with that which is plastic; dealing with dreams that come true on the instant, where one thing good and right to have is always at hand.

We are to see that the wish is already fulfilled, for all creation is at hand in the nothing. To grasp this simple yet stupendous idea is to live a life of charm and freedom. It was the wonderful Jesus who uttered the covenant, "*All* things are possible to him that believeth." When we can believe that all things are possible, then they are possible. And this is easy to believe when we perceive *how* and *why* all things are possible.

To even faintly perceive the nothingness of creation, hence the *possibility of anything, of everything on the instant,* is to feel a release, an emancipation not equal to expression.

If you have a wish like the selling of a house or owning of a car or whatever the wish might be, know that this wish is fulfilled on the instant, for your wish is like the object (image) that stands in the mirror (mind). When you see an object in a mirror, you know very well that there is an original standing before the mirror, do you not? And when you have a wish, you may be sure that the original or the *fulfillment* of that wish already exists, else this wish or reflection would not be taking place in your mind (mirror).

All things in this world such as cars, houses, money, are but reflections of divine realities, hence they are infinite and unlimited in expression. The man in the night dream as related before, wished money, and he could have it because of the fifty dollars that he had in the day experience. So when we wish cars, homes and money, we can have them, because we have abundance and joys and harmonies and satisfaction in heaven.

In relating my demonstration of the white house with green shutters, a student asked, "But how did you know that a house such as you wanted actually existed on this plane? Supposing that what you wanted was the impossible?" My answer was, "Because I had a picture of it."

Now, if on your mantel there stood a photograph of a country home, anyone would know without questioning you that the original existed, for how could it be possible for you to have a picture unless there were an original of which this was the reflection or likeness? Thus when you have *decided* desires, you may be sure that the fulfillment or the original already exists for you, otherwise you would not be in possession of the photograph, the picture in your mind.

Many, however, are so prone to change their feelings and desires that demonstration becomes impossible. Today they may want a certain thing, and tomorrow the wish is changed for something else, or they are not really certain whether it would be best for them to have such a thing or not.

Now, when you wish to demonstrate creation, you must be certain, you must be strong and unwavering. You take seeds and plant them in the ground, the nothing, and duly they spring forth, or are externalized. So also plant your wish in the nothing—in the unknown, or mirror—and surely it will be reflected or externalized for you. When a demonstration is rightly made, every detail is satisfactory, and harmony is demonstrated for everyone concerned.

It is not enough for us to declare that we are spiritual beings, not enough for us to assert that we are living in a perfect world, but we must *feel* it. Spiritual consciousness is not emotion of the mind but is an inner feeling, a full, deep sense of joy, peace, fulfillment.

Since man is himself the fact of Life, then the joy, the peace, the ecstasy stands upon nothing external for support but comes from within.

The place of understanding is that man has *already* attained success, even before he attempts to reach it. This is indeed a new evolution. Man is not to ascend, evolve, develop, attain success, but on the contrary, it is as though man were wrapped in a veil and he must pierce this covering. It is as though man were walking through a great wilderness and must find himself. Man must rend the veil. He must strip off the disguise. He must "come to himself." He must "stand still and behold."

When man is to demonstrate supply, demonstrate health, demonstrate joy, he is not to be taken off and educated and instructed how to acquire and construct these things that he desires. He is not to seek for health and wealth as though he would add these to himself like a cloak or a garment which he would put on, but the New Day, the

Angel of Insight, shows man that he is to begin *at the end.* He is to arrive before he starts. He is to see no distance from man to Truth, no distance from the beginning to the end.

I possess it *now! Now* are we the Sons of Glory, the Sons of Wealth! *Now* is come the kingdom of God and the power of His glory!

Out of the mirror springs anything that is before the mirror, and out of the mirror of clear mind springs the nothingness called material creation— houses, lands, jewels, business opportunities. My world of fortune is within. It is not dependent upon certain cities, certain beliefs, certain people. The finished attainment, the possession of all fortune is within man.

In the midst of our sickness, we are health. In the midst of our poverty, we are wealth. In the midst of our sorrow, we are joy. Let us see and acknowledge ourselves as we *are.* Let us claim our dominion and power and glory from on high. Let us know that we are not to be given a perfect body some time after we depart from this world; we are not to be given power and health and joy some day in some other future world—but *now* are we clothed in the body of shining light; *now* are we crowned with that glory greater than the sun; *now* are we the possessors of the wealth of the whole universe. This is not human evolution, but this is *divine revelation.*

Let us approach this instruction, this truth, as though it were true, as though we believed in it with all our hearts and souls. Let us listen to it as though we were listening to the most exquisite of music, as though we were walking through places of indescribable beauty. Let us *feel* this truth to be *true.* Let us see that it is not a question of attaining, but a question of accepting.

There is no long journey before us, no world to be conquered, no fortune to be earned, but we are there before we start, and that which is last is also first. Let this Truth come upon man, tearing the veil from his eyes, lifting the yoke from his shoulders and the burden from his heart. Such revelation is that blaze of glory which causes man to forget his fears, forget his doubts, forget his worries of the material world, for he is looking into the divine Mirror, the light of Glory, *beholding himself face to face.*

A woman sat at the side of a teacher, for the first time listening to the story of perfect man, the revelation of glory and wholeness now and here. This woman had much trouble with her eyesight and had worn glasses for many years, not being able to read without them. Upon hearing the word of Life and wholeness, swiftly she tore off her glasses.

Why, if this were true, she did not need glasses! What need the Son of the Almighty for such appendage! Dancing with the delight of a child, she ran to the bookcase, lifting out a dictionary of unusually small type, and seating herself again at the side of the teacher, she opened the book, reading aloud instantly anywhere, any place where her glance happened to fall.

Blessed are they who believe, for they shall receive. Blessed are they who upon hearing the Word *act upon it*. Blessed are they who understand that the universe of fortune is not external, but is *within*, that one may have all the reflection he wishes *because of its nothingness*.

We do not say that the world is perfect so that it will thereby become perfect, but because it is prefect we state that it is perfect. If you say to one, "You are wealth," with the belief that your words will make him wealthy, you are in ignorance. You are to state that a person is health, is wealth, because it is so. You are to state your perception, *your recognition of the Truth*. In this way the ignorance in the mind, the veil that seems to cover one is consumed, is melted away, is returned to nothingness.

To understand the nothingness of materiality does not encourage extravagance or wastefulness, nor does it create in one the notion of intemperance or the misuse of anything. Because of the realities in heaven, it is right that we have their symbols on earth; yet such experience on earth but glorifies and exalts one, causing him to rejoice not over possessions or ownership, but to rejoice over the allness, the omnipresence, the joy and the glory of Truth and the true experience of man in heavenly abundance of all good, *now and here.*

CHAPTER IX

Individuality and Identity

To see that while man is *one*, still man has individuality and identity that is never lost but is eternally preserved is a most important point to grasp and understand spiritually.

Probably most of us in the past have believed ourselves to be material beings living in a material world, and after a time many of us believed that we were mental beings living in a mental world; but now a fuller vision has come that we are spiritual beings living in a spiritual world.

Absolute Science presents spiritual man as individual being whose identity is never lost nor is it absorbed into Deity, but it is perpetual, uninterrupted, eternal.

There seem to be many beings, separate beings, whereas there is only one. With our minds we see many, but with our insight, with our spiritual consciousness we see unity, oneness. God is *infinite* and so includes all in one.

It is a great step for us to see and understand this, for how can one demonstrate his spirituality except he recognize and understand it?

What we need to spiritualize is not man but our sense of man. From God the Father, infinite Spirit, proceeds all individuality, all being, hence the perfection and infinity of such individuality. There is but one idea of a flower, for instance, but the multiplicity of this idea reveals its infinity.

Now, material personality is not individual man. As the sense of materiality disappears, the spiritual individuality appears. That which is mortal, that which belongs to a dream world, that which has beginning and end is not man; still, what our actual spiritual individuality is we have yet to more clearly perceive.

Sin and sickness are no part of man but in belief obscure man. It was Jesus who with pure spiritual insight saw man as he *is*. The dream can call itself a dreamer, but as the dream passes, man is seen as he is — perfect, individual being. To annihilate through insight the belief in mortal man, the belief in sin, sickness, death; to annihilate the belief of any power, any being other than the One, brings to light perfect man *at hand*.

Man has been called the "idea" of God, or God's perfect idea, and it has been taught that God's infinite ideas are the "children of God" or sons and daughters. Right here a simple illustration may help explain the relationship of God and man more clearly. If an author writes a book of fiction, he has perhaps many characters or ideas in the book, and the relationship between God and man is similar to that between an author and his characters.

Each character in the book of fiction springs from the mind of the author; each is his idea, and while the author has infinite ideas or characters, still every single one is *himself.* A character in the book could truly state, "I of mine own self can do nothing, for as the author thinketh, so I performeth, and when you see me you see the author, for there is nothing to be but the author. I live in the author and the author lives in me."

It can be seen that there would be no author without the characters in the book, and there would be no characters in the book without the author—symbolizing oneness, unity. The author may have an infinite number of characters, yet each one is the author and is nothing else. Is this not so?

Now, it is this way with perfect God and perfect man. God is the *unseen* Author (Father) and man is the seen character. Man is the perfect character written in the Book of Life. He is in one sense the expression, or manifestation or idea of God, while in another sense he is God, for God is *all* there is to him. *The fact is that there is nothing besides God!*

When God is perceived as a *trinity*, then man can be better understood. This trinity is Father, Son, Holy Ghost—Self, Man, Revelation, forever a trinity in unity, forever the one Being, inseparable, indivisible, indissoluble.

In the Book of Life move the characters called the children of God. They are one being expressed as infinite ideas. The life, substance, intelligence of each character comes from the one Source, hence their oneness. The characters in this Book of Life have individuality and identity which is forever preserved, perfect, eternal, immortal.

This was the mission of Jesus Christ — to demonstrate, show forth the ideal man so that man would recognize *himself*, would acknowledge his Selfhood to be God! So that man would perceive that inasmuch as God is the writer of the Book of Life, the Author of the universe, He writes in it nothing but joy and love and good and harmony. Hence, all trouble comes not from divine Mind but is wholly falsity, and man must so recognize and understand.

God is one and man is one, but it is the same One! God is infinite and man is infinite, but it is the same Infinity!

In belief we see personality rather than individuality. As the former passes away to sense, the real and eternal becomes known to us.

Between man's sense of personality and his individuality there wages that warfare that will end in man's discovery of Himself—his birthless, deathless and forever harmonious Being. Truth will destroy all belief in a selfhood apart from the One.

Man, the character in the Book of Life, is a celestial being, eternally harmonious and individual in the spiritual universe, and he must be so recognized and understood. Absolute Science by no means annihilates one's individuality and identity, but on the contrary shows the impossibility of its loss or interruption.

Man does not lose his identity even in this world, as he seemingly passes through the successive bodies from the cradle to the grave, nor will the passing through the experience called death touch in any way his perpetual and changeless identity and individuality.

Who can describe the reality of ideal man? "And his face did shine as the sun, and his raiment was white as the light." Spiritual sense belongs to spiritual man, and this ideal, spiritual and individual man is perfect in body as well as in spirit.

The Father came into this world in the form of the *Son — Jesus Christ.* Jesus acknowledged this relationship, this oneness, when he said, "He that seeth me seeth the Father," that is, we are the same being. "God was manifest in the flesh." (1 Tim. 3:16).

Who being in the form of God thought it not robbery to be equal with God. But he took upon himself the form of a servant and was made in the likeness of men. (Phil. 2: 6, 7).

Ever since "the beginning" it was planned that a redeemer, a Christ or savior would come into this world. He came. He assumed the guise of a human being, yet his conception was immaculate.

Behold a virgin shall be with child, and shall bring forth a son, and they shall call his name Emmanuel, which being interpreted is, God with us (Matt. 1: 23).

God is a trinity—a tri-unity. God the *Father* is infinite Soul, Self, the unseen, invisible Life, Intelligence, Substance, Power, Love. God the *Son* is perfect man, perfect character, and such expression is infinite because of the infinity of the Father. God the *Holy Ghost* is the understanding, the revelation, the blazing mirror of illumination, showing man *Himself.*

There would be no man without God. There would be no God without man. You can never sever into parts or particles that which is *one* and that which is indivisible.

To understand Jesus Christ is to understand perfect God and perfect man. This is what Jesus came to exemplify. One cannot receive this insight, this understanding of Jesus Christ from another. It must come from *within*. It is written on the supernal page: "No one can say that Jesus is Lord but by the Holy Ghost."

It is the light, the inspiration, the glory of God which breathes upon one the marvel that Jesus was Christ and Christ is God. No one can grasp this mystic wonder with his mind or with his senses. It must come to him through divine illumination, which is the Holy Ghost.

Once one sees the deity of Jesus Christ, sees the oneness of God and man through divine revelation, he can never be turned aside from this knowledge. It is ever within him like a burning fire. It was Jesus who showed us that heaven is here, and it is for us to take the mote from our eyes so that we may behold as Soul beholds, that we may see as God sees.

It is asked, "Are we exactly the same as Jesus, or was Jesus different? Why did he say that we could do the same works that he did?"

Jesus entered this world with a mission: "God sent his Son into the world that the world through him might be saved."

Jesus came taking the form of man, yet consciously knowing the nothingness of a fiction world and the reality and allness of heaven at hand. For the reason that he knew this was he able to deliver this truth to others. He knew that there is no difference in life, in substance, in being.

Now, it is as we understand him that we, too, see that his life is actually our life, his being is actually our being, since there is but *one Life and one Being.*

If we have the insight to clearly recognize and understand this, we can then perceive that when Jesus healed the sick, *we* healed the sick; when he raised the dead, *we* raised the dead. The works that he did, *we* did, for there *is* but One—*there is no other!*

In this glorious vision of the One, love pours into our hearts, overflowing with praise and wonder. Losing all sense of possession, of ownership, of egotism, of selfishness and vainglory, we bask in the joy and in the glory of the one Lord Jesus Christ, in our midst and in our hearts, as our life and as our being.

If still you cannot perceive clearly the oneness of man, the oneness of being, then consider some parables and illustrations. In the night dream in which everything that we make and create seems external to us, it is really not external at all. If I create cities, rivers, streets, people, what are these but myself? I am the only being in the dream. Is this not so? If I dream that I am talking with a stranger, holding conversation with him, since he came from no source other than from me, then he is myself, and in the final analysis there is nothing at all in my dream but myself.

Now, the same thing can be said about an author and his book. The characters which he creates have no existence outside himself'. He it is who speaks, lives and acts through each of his characters. There would be no characters without the author, hence the nothingness of the characters and the allness of the one being—the author.

The teachings of truth tell us that Jesus is the author and finisher, the first and the last; that Jesus is Christ and Christ is God, and that the universe is the Book of Life. We can easily see that as the characters in any fiction book are actually the author, so the characters in the universe (the Book of Life) are expressions of the Author and such expression is called perfect man.

Since the Author is perfect and knows nothing but perfection, then His characters would have to be perfect, would they not? Because of the constitution of His nature, He could not or would not have any idea of imperfection about Himself or about His characters nor see any evil in Himself or in His characters.

Perfect man, perfect character, is none other than the one Being, for the one Being is *all* there is!

The One is the writer of the Book. *The One* is the characters in the Book. *The One* is the book itself! *The One* is the *All-in-all!*

For ages the task of all religions has been to unite God and man, but *how can you unite that which cannot be separated, that which has never been less than one Being?* God and man are one Being, the same Being, as the author and his book characters are the same being.

This is why men have been called "the children of God," the "images of God," the "sons and daughters of God." For God is *all* there is to them.

Now, we cannot think of God as expressing anything in His characters other than what He is, can we? Thus, the characters called mankind show His changelessness, His omnipotence, His wonder and His perfection. How utterly impossible then for this perfect man, the God-character, to be sick, to be weak, to be poor, to be deaf, for how could he unless God were causing this? God does not and cannot look upon evil for the reason that there is none in His being. And His being is All-Being, hence, there is no evil at all.

Now, since God is All, then the character *man* must be included in this All, for how can there be All and something besides? There cannot. This is a delicate subject to handle, yet can be easily grasped and understood if presented clearly and if one is spiritually minded. One who has this understanding does not voice the statement, "Man is God," nor the statement, "I am God." If one understands the truth, he will know the position of God, man and the universe. Jesus, of course, understood this and sometimes spoke of himself as the "Father" and again as the "Son."

We should see this clearly so as to express ourselves in correct language. When we mean the *Self*, we should not say "man," but we should say *I* or He. When we are speaking of the individual character, meaning *Soul and body*, we should then say "Man." When we mean merely the *body* of man then let us say body. Let us remember to speak plainly and clearly, making it easy for others not so advanced as we are to understand. It is wisdom to use simple, easy language when speaking of spiritual things, for this is most easily comprehended.

We know of students who object to being called "reflections," and they have a right to do so. *We* are not reflections, nor is the character "Man" a reflection. A reflection is that which has no life, substance or power, but images it forth, and such reflection is the *body* of man. The body images forth action, strength, health, beauty and so on. When one is speaking of the "reflection," if he is speaking with understanding, he means the *body*.

As the author of a fiction book is the life of his characters, so God is *our* very life. This God is the Soul or Self. Soul or Self is the I AM, is the one and only Being, is the Writer of the Book of Life. It was truly said of the peerless Jesus that he was "God made flesh," and they who saw and understood and loved him, saw not mortal man but saw God manifested in the flesh, even as they proclaimed. They knew that a being of love, of peace, of power, of glory could be none other than the One, the only being, God.

Seeing Jesus in this true light, they did not see him in a dream world, but they saw him in an actual world, in the true world, in the only world.

Did not the understanding Jesus assert— "Inasmuch as ye have done it unto the least of these, ye have done it unto me." This is a glorious confession of unity, of oneness. His life, your life, my life, the life of the greatest and the life of the smallest, all as *one* Being, the *same* Being!

Let us be ready always to acknowledge and to praise Truth:

I love to acknowledge the Truth!
I love to acknowledge one Power, one Substance, one Being!
I love to acknowledge the goodness, the love, the glory of God, at hand!

I love to acknowledge that my heart is fixed on the peace and the power of the One!

"Come unto Me, all ye who are weary and sad," calls the voice of Truth in this world today. Yet how many think, "Perhaps tomorrow or next week or next year, I will be ready." It is like the one who sits down to read a book of fiction. He makes himself comfortable, opens the book and soon is lost in the story. He no longer hears the tick of the clock on the mantel; the fire in the grate burns itself out; he forgets that it is time to eat, time to retire, for he is lost in the romance, in the fiction that is absorbing his attention.

Someone speaks to him, calls his name. He answers, "Do not bother me. Wait a while. Let me alone."

And so in this world, there are those lost in the so-called pleasures of money, sin, happiness. When they hear the call, "Come unto Me. Come, learn of spiritual things," do they not answer, "Let us alone. We are enjoying this romance. Wait a little longer"? If they but knew it, the romance does not have to be set aside, the fiction does not have to be cut off, the pleasures are not to be thrown away when one accepts the spiritual life. But they are seen and accepted as just what they are—fiction only, hence harmless. Vision is raised into the perception of higher pleasures and joys of higher order.

Many are there who need just a bit of clearer vision, just a little more faith, just a little stronger hold. Well might they sing the hymn—

Almost persuaded now to believe;
Almost persuaded Truth to receive.

When this notion of another, this notion of a separate selfhood is seen as falsity, then Soul worships Soul, Self glimpses Self, Being understands Being, and Thy kingdom is come on earth as it is in heaven.

Thus it is that when you read a book or read words of Truth that bring forth in you the spirit of worship and adoration, the spirit of love and devotion, of freedom and unspeakable joy, you should rise in the strength and courage of your vision, and you should recognize that it is not another to whom you must give glory and credit, not another whose light is shining upon you, enlightening you, *for there is no other.* There is but the One! The books of Truth which you read were written by Soul, Self, the one and only Being, Ourself.

Throughout the ages Truth has apparently dawned upon the universe gradually, line upon line, precept upon precept, here a little, there a little. The vision that there is One only to whom glory and honor belong does not come to us in our first fresh glimpse of understanding, for then we would not be able to grasp it. Then we blessed *others,* we praised *others,* not knowing that all others are *Ourself.* Then we gave credit to others, we sang their names abroad, we spoke of them as though they were apart from us and were specially spiritually endowed. When we were children in vision, we understood as children, but as our vision enlarges we have a fuller perception of Being.

In heaven every knee is bowed to Truth, and every heart confesseth the Christ as the Self universal. It is only when we see through a glass darkly in this human dream experience that we seem to see some beings as true worshippers and others as false worshippers, some as sinners and some as saints. Finally it will be seen that no matter how many delusions or dream existences one may encounter, it is impossible to deceive or delude the Self, and man will see his Reality, his Self as It *is.*

Now that it is presented to us clearly the oneness of life, we understand that as we look into a mirror and see not another but see ourself, so it is that when we look into the great mirror, the Book of Life, we see not another, but we behold *Ourself*—the *one* Self. Past visions, devices called unfoldment, are then set aside and we see face to face.

Take an example called man, a sinner. We will suppose that he is in prison, held by the mental law and sentenced to die because of having taken the life of another man. Suppose that this man, called a murderer, knows nothing of Truth, of God. How are you to approach him in order to instruct him in Spirit and help him? Do you see that you may of necessity have at first to resort to the device of "line upon line," the device that has been used throughout the ages, imparting Truth to man gradually?

Suppose that one should say, "I will not use device, but I will approach him as one who knows, as one who understands." Acting upon this impulsion, he speaks to the prisoner, who has never been taught about God, as follows:

"You never killed another man, for man cannot die. You never saw a man who was born, for man was never born. You or anyone else never saw a man sick or in pain or in want, for there never has been such a man. Man was never born and man has never died, and no one has ever been known to see a dead man. There are no hospitals, no prisons, no cemeteries and man never saw any. There are no changes such as morning and night, good and bad, right and wrong, happiness and unhappiness. There are no laws and none to enforce a law. There is no such thing as sin, no such thing as punishment, no killing or dying, and you are now a changeless, perfect being in heaven, enjoying eternal bliss and glory."

Do you think that the one called prisoner would believe this? And according to the authority, Jesus, there would then be no hope for him, no help, for the supernal Word reads: "If thou canst believe, all things are possible to him that believeth." Can you see how important then is *belief*? If the prisoner could not believe, he could not be helped, and he would then have to pay the mental penalty of his sentence.

Nevertheless, there is a way called "conversion," and the lines read, "Repent ye therefore, and be converted, that your sins may be blotted out."

Then if the prisoner is told that God is Love, if he is shown such mercy that reaches and touches his heart, he will be melted; he will repent; he will *believe*. Acting then upon his belief, he enters as it were a new country.

He becomes vitally interested in spiritual things, and in belief he travels on and on until finally he comes to the vision of the one and only Being, the same in every breast, and the Book of Life written from beginning to end with the joys of perfect, changeless Selfhood.

As clearer perception dawns upon us, we lay aside toys and fictions, and we see plainly with understanding. We can look back to the time when the general belief on this plane was an after-heaven-and-hell. It was then supposed that after leaving this earth one would at some future period find himself either in the place of eternal rest and peace called *heaven,* or else in another place of burning and torture called *hell.* Therefore, many chose to be good, chose not to do evil because they did not like the idea of a later hell.

Through the belief of a hell hereafter, they gave up the practice of many things which otherwise they would not have given up. Not because of the love of Truth, the love of God, but through *fear of evil,* through fear of later punishment, men chose to be good, to live better lives.

Later, as more insight dawned into the hearts of mankind, the notion of a personal devil and an external hell were laid aside by many, and it was presented to the world that all the evil there is exists in one's own mind. It was taught that one can experience hell right here on earth; that one suffers because of ignorance and sin and that this suffering will last as long as the sin continues, thus it is self-inflicted. Many then chose to be good, chose to think right thoughts, *for fear of evil results* if they continued with evil thinking.

We hear even today of the call coming from the pulpit, "Come, lay your sins at Jesus' feet. Come, *believing* that Jesus will wash away your sins," and marvelous conversions follow. A man, called sinner, steeped in the depths of hell, suddenly reaches out for spiritual help. Turning away from the calls of this world, he reaches the altar. Hearing the sweet words of love and comfort, the heavenly promise that, "Though your sins be red like crimson, they shall he as wool," and weeping with mingled joy and sorrow, he rises up a new man. He went to that altar with the belief that he was a sinner, weak, unloved. He rises up with the belief that he left his sins at the altar; that he is now a child of God; that he is strong because he feels the love of God in his heart.

And who shall say that this man has not reason to rejoice? *All things are possible; only believe.* The sins which he left at the altar were not gathered up in a basket and thrown away. No one saw them. No one picked them up. Yet it was the same to him as though he *actually* left them there, for now the burden has been rolled away from his heart; he walks upright, he looks man in the face, he is conscious of new life, new hope, new glory.

Then someday he shall know that man is a changeless being, that sinning in a fiction world is the same as not sinning at all, that man, the glory of God, *cannot* sin, for he is like God.

"He cannot sin, because he is born of God" (1 John 3: 9).

Then man will no longer turn away from evil because of the belief in its somethingness and his fear of it. He will no longer endeavor to stop thinking wrong thoughts because of his fear of the results; but lo, he will be good *because he loves to be good*, because he loves Truth. He will stop sinning *because he beholds the nothingness of evil!*

Let us bring our hearts, our affections to the altar of divine Love. Let us say often:

I love the Truth!

I love the fact that life is unchangeable, immutable, everlasting.

I love to know that I am a trinity—Self, Son, Understanding.

I love to think of the Self as mighty, majestic, unconquerable.

I love to think of man as the Son shining forth the love and joy of Being.

I love to think of Understanding as coming to man like blazing light, like shining gold, like fiery flame.

I love to think of heaven as here, at hand, a land of beauty, aglow with the divine energy of Life.

> I love to perceive the nothingness of matter and mind and personality.
> I love to behold the unity and allness of the *One.*

Now, one might say, "Yes, the life and spirit are the same in us all, but surely the forms are different. The form of the child is not the same as the form of the adult." Yes, they are alike; they are the same.

To illustrate: One has a pan of dough before him, and in baking this he places some of it in the form of biscuits and some in the form of bread. Now, when they are all baked, when they are taken from the oven, the substance of the form called *biscuit* is the very same, is identical with the substance in the form of the *bread,* is it not? The salt, sugar, milk, water, yeast are identically the same, whether in biscuit or bread.

Now, should the biscuit look at the bread and think, "I am not bread; I am biscuit," you can see the folly of it, can you not? The biscuit is the bread and the bread is the biscuit in substance and in form, and there is no difference whatever. Gold is gold whether it is shaped into a ring or a bracelet. We alone place a difference; assume a different value to one than the other. The paper used in a fifty-dollar bill is exactly the same as that used in a one-dollar bill. But a different value has been placed upon them, has been agreed upon, yet their substance is the same.

This will show us clearly that every man is every other man; that one thing is every other thing. The estimate, the value which man places upon the thing, has nothing whatever to do with that which it is. All lives are one *Life*. All forms are one element.

The mind is that instrument which manufactures delusion. It looks at one thing and reports something else. It looks at perfection and reports imperfection. It looks at that which is nothing and calls it something. It looks at unity and sees duality. It looks at oneness and reports separation. The mind trembles without cause, doubts without reason and disbelieves because of its own ignorance.

Let us place Ourself in authority over the mind, instructing it to speak truth, to love good, to see perfection, to reflect intelligence. Let us teach it to see that underneath all appearances is the reality. Underneath the idea *money* is abundance; underneath the idea *home* is protection; underneath the idea *work* is the unlabored action of the divine Life. And so on.

There is no evil world. There is no world of pain and bondage. There is no world of dimension and limitation. The world of glory exists right here, a world in which we are now living and moving, and any mind that perceives illusions, such as pain and evil, is totally without foundation in Truth. The body that we now have is the perfect embodiment of Truth. Not the body that one may think he has, but the body that one actually has.

Let us see reality, truth, about ourselves and the universe—even while we seem to be in a material world—rather than imagine that we must leave this world because of its unreality. There is discernment beyond the insight that all is mental. One first sees the world as material, and then he takes it and shifts it into a mental world; but he has still a higher vision to grasp—he has still to perceive that *a mental thing has no more actuality than a material thing and that all that is real and true and lasting is Truth and Its manifestation.*

There is no need putting off a demonstration. There is no need delaying illumination.

No man knoweth the hour when Truth shall break through this earthly dream existence so that all so-called human beings will confess their true being, but this we know, *that in heaven there are no unbelievers!*

In heaven there are none who do not confess the finished kingdom, at hand! There are none who do not acknowledge the Absolute Christ within! There are none who do not demonstrate in

His name! There are none who see other than the *One!*

FINIS

About the Author

Lillian DeWaters was born in 1883 and lived in Stamford, Connecticut. She grew up with a Christian Science background and in her early teens began to study metaphysics and on that same day to seriously study the Bible. "It was from the Bible that I learned to turn from all else to God direct.... What stood out to me above all else was the fact presented, that when they turned to God they received Light and Revelation; they walked and talked with God; and they found peace and freedom."

She published several books while actively within the Christian Science organization and then in 1924 she had an awakening experience when it was as though a veil was parted and Truth was revealed to her. From that point she began to receive numerous unfoldments which led to her separation from the Christian Science organization.

She created her own publishing company and became a prolific writer with over 30 books published in 15 languages. She was a well-known teacher who taught regularly at the Waldorf Astoria in New York and she was sought after as a healer throughout the world.

All of her books are based on her inner unfoldments of Divine Truth with each text revealing specifics of Truth that serious students will immediately recognize as spiritual treasures.

CPSIA information can be obtained
at www.ICGtesting.com
Printed in the USA
LVOW12s1437231017
553448LV00001B/206/P